D1206243

*Law in Society Series*

CRIME AND CONFLICT

A Study of Law and Society

# Crime and Conflict

A STUDY OF LAW AND SOCIETY

## HAROLD E. PEPINSKY

*Law in Society Series*

edited by
C. M. CAMPBELL and P. N. P. WILES

ACADEMIC PRESS, INC.   New York   San Francisco

A Subsidiary of Harcourt Brace Jovanovich, Publishers

1976

© Harold E. Pepinsky 1976

All rights reserved. No part of this publication may be reproduced, stored in a retrieval system, or transmitted in any form or by any means, electronic, mechanical, photocopying, recording or otherwise without the prior written permission of the copyright holder.

First published in 1976 by Martin Robertson & Company Ltd., 17 Quick Street, London N1 8HL, and by Academic Press, Inc., 111 Fifth Avenue, New York, N.Y. 10003.

ISBN 0-12-550050-5

LCCCN 75-45758

Set by Santype (Coldtype) Ltd., Salisbury
Printed and bound in Britain at The Pitman Press, Bath

K
5029
.p46

# CONTENTS

149140     WITHDRAWN

EMORY & HENRY LIBRARY

EGORY & HENRY LIBRARY

# INTRODUCTORY NOTE

The concept of *rational formalism* has become the accepted notion for describing the nature of law in modern societies. Whilst in the work of more sensitive writers the relation between formal rationality and social structure has been one of detailed historical contingency, nevertheless a version of the sociological convergence thesis has commonly created a necessary link between formal rationality and industrialisation and modernity. The result has sometimes been that whilst the consequences, both intended and unintended, of legal rationalism have been disparagingly chartered, they have been defined as inevitable consequences of industrial society. Social theories about law of this kind have therefore had both an unreal and pessimistic quality. Unreal in that they seemed to argue against the possibility of using law as an instrument of social change in anything but trivial cases, whilst those involved in the production and reception of such ideas were at the same time frequently those most actively involved in trying to use law to achieve change. Pessimistic in that their doom-laden historicism often appeared to be reversible only by destroying the very basis and structure of modern societies.

Harold Pepinsky's book, in examining the relationships between rationality, legal formalism and social structure and change, has the advantage of developing a theory which, whilst critical, is neither unreal nor ultimately pessimistic. Pepinsky has set himself the task of examining the precise nature of legal rationality and formalism in the United States in particular, and modern, western capitalist societies more generally. The advantage of this analysis is that it allows him not only to discuss how this legal structure is a product of that social and ideological order, but also how they continue to interact and become dependent upon each other. The resulting theory allows law a place as a potentially powerful instrument of social change.

Harold Pepinsky's work grows out of that period of North American academic endeavour of the 1960's which sought the basis for a new political humanitarian radicalism, as an alternative to the horrors and moral bankruptcy of Vietnam, racial riots etc., by exploring the nature of social solidarity and its relation to law. That period raised once again the intellectual problem which had fascinated the great European social theorists of the nineteenth century, but it brought to the problem a new sense of urgency. At times that very political urgency appeared as theoretical naivety or even crudeness to European readers steeped in the classic debates over industrialisation, capitalism and social solidarity and control. However the 'new conflict theorists', as they became known, did direct a new generation of American social theorists towards fresh problems and perspectives. Pepinsky's work belongs to this second generation when over-crude notions of 'conflict' have been replaced by more developed social theories which, at the same time, maintain a radical commitment to social change.

The nature of this new American radicalism has, at its best, a concern for the practicalities and details of change which is rarely matched in European writing. Pepinsky is not satisfied with examining the effects of legal rationality and formalism on his own society, but in order to explore the practicality of change, carries out a comparative analysis with the People's Republic of China with its very different legal and social system. There is throughout a concern to demonstrate that the policy proposals which conclude the book are based both on an articulated social theory, and on some evidence that such changes may be practical for an industrialised society. Works of social theory which are aimed at creating social change necessarily have an unfinished quality about them: their veracity depends upon their implementation. Yet for those of us interested in the social nature of law Pepinsky's book allows us to conceive of law as one means of achieving such change.

C.M.C.
P.N.P.W.

# ACKNOWLEDGEMENTS

Perhaps one gets jaded after writing several books. For this, my first, I have been overwhelmed at how much input from others has helped me to construct my thoughts and put them on paper. Much of my work has been stimulated over the years in the intellectual companionship of Harold B. and Pauline Pepinsky. I am indebted to Harold B. Pepinsky for having pushed me to try to clarify my written expression. Pauline Pepinsky has developed concepts of cultural variations in the meaning of freedom and social control which have influenced me greatly. Long standing debts of gratitude go also to Magnus Hedberg and a number of other Scandinavians who fourteen years ago introduced me to new cultural notions of freedom and social control. I hope they will forgive my failure to mention all of them by name.

During my undergraduate study of China and the Chinese language, Harriet Mills gave me such an intensive introduction to Chinese Communist writings in that language that I virtually felt them come to life. I thank also those scholars in the field who helped guide my study of Chinese law, notably Jerry Cohen and Victor Li.

As I recall, it was Lloyd Ohlin who first made me consider the possibility that people could use various criteria besides the law itself to determine whether crime had occurred. I am indebted to Marvin Wolfgang, among many other students of criminology at the University of Pennsylvania, and to Harold Finestone, among other students of deviance at the University of Minnesota, for helping me to discover more about this problem, particularly in reference to the way in which police make official decisions that offences have occurred. More than anyone else I have the men of the Sixth Police Precinct in Minneapolis to thank for teaching me about American police decision-making. Others with far more first-hand experience in American criminal justice than I, including especially Fred Villaume, have helped me greatly to make sense of what I have seen and read about the American criminal-justice system in general.

My thanks are due to colleagues and students at Albany for their support and valuable feedback. Among many, Les Wilkins, Graeme Newman, Jack Kress, Travis Hirschi, and Joanne Joseph have helped indicate where points could be clarified. Dick Myren has been my closest critic and a careful editor.

With financial support from the National Science Foundation, I was able to obtain the valuable services of Joe Calpin, and Mark and Barbara Robarge have provided literary advice and encouragement. As co-editor of the 'Law in Society' Series, Paul Wiles has made consistently sensible suggestions for substantive revision of the manuscript and David Martin has helped to make the task of getting the book together a pleasure, and his house editors have provided invaluable assistance.

Special thanks go to Bill Chambliss for his encouragement and advice.

Much needed, competent assistance in typing has been provided by Helen Stenzel, Jo Anne DeSilva, Karen Mitchell, Rita Palumbo and Sue Shields.

The dedication of the book is to my constant companion, my inspiration — my wife, Jill — who more than anyone else helps me build my ideas and put them together.

The contributions of countless others are also appreciated. I can only hope that the study as I now report it begins to match the measure of help I have received in producing it.

Harold E. Pepinsky
School of Criminal Justice
State University of New York
Albany, New York
1975

To my Kotie

# INTRODUCTION[1]

Social conditions in the United States today are leading toward a revolution in thinking about jurisprudence, or guiding philosophy of law. Seemingly, there have been a number of such revolutions in Western history already, from 'schools' of 'natural law', 'formalism', 'cultural and historical schools', 'utilitarianism' and 'sociological jurisprudence' to 'legal realism'. And yet these 'schools' share an assumption that remains with us to the present. The assumption is that the criterion by which influence of the law is measured is the extent of compliance with the law's literal terms.

To the extent that an American police officer is influenced by the law of *Miranda*, he will warn any suspect he takes into custody of the suspect's rights against self-incrimination and to counsel, and the officer will immediately cease interrogation if the suspect expresses a wish not to answer questions. To the extent that a private citizen is influenced by the law, he will not drive another's car without the owner's permission. If the officer or the citizen does not abide by these terms of law, it is not *because* of or *with reference* to the law, but *in spite of* the law.

To members of any of the 'schools' of jurisprudence mentioned above, it would be absurd to say of an officer who cajoles a confession out of a suspect without giving the *Miranda* warnings or of a citizen who drives off a stranger's car that each is conforming to the dictates of the law. In traditional terms, it would be paradoxical to believe that one has been influenced by the law. At best, a transgressor can 'rationalise', 'neutralise', 'normalise' or otherwise 'distort' the violation in an attempt to explain it away. The traditional assumption is that the law has failed to shape the behaviour of a defendant for which criminal or civil guilt has been attached.

What a bind this has put us in! We have been left to treat those we

1

discover to have violated the law as 'unreasonable', 'irrational', 'insane', or blind to the terms of the law. We have tried to induce reasonableness, rationality and compliance by surgery, corporal punishment, humiliation, confinement, labour, training, supervision and other 'rewards' and 'punishments'. The harder we try to induce conformity to the law where conformity does not exist, the more we seem to fail. The closer we look for failure to conform to the law, the more instances we find. In the United States, as long ago as 1947, Wallerstein and Wyle found, among a large random sample of adults in New York State, that when interviewed over 90 per cent of the sample acknowledged having committed offences as adults for which they could have been jailed or imprisoned, at a rate of eighteen offences per man and eleven offences per woman. As the years go by, rates of both official and private crime are found to continue to rise. If illicit behaviour is increasing disproportionately, it follows that licit behaviour is proportionately decreasing, which, by traditional notions of jurisprudence, leads to the conclusion that the effect of criminal law is attenuating.

This conclusion is untenable not only because of its pessimism, but because of its own absurdity. The conclusion implies that the influence of law on the behaviour of officials and private citizens is *negatively* correlated with the volume of written law and the number of those who are employed in its administration. The conclusion even implies a negative correlation between the size of law and legal apparatus on the one hand and reliance of citizens on formal legal mechanisms on the other. As court dockets increase, the number of lawyers working for citizens grows astronomically and the police are regularly called for more and more matters such as the disturbance caused by a neighbour's stereo. In the name of parsimony, a jurisprudence is called for which proceeds from the empirical premise that as the influence of formal written law and its administration in our society grow, the rates of violations of the law can be expected to increase concomitantly.

The crux of the task of developing a new jurisprudence is to isolate commonalities of what we now conceive to be antithetical behaviours — those typically termed 'compliant' and those deemed to be 'violative'. It has previously seemed obvious that compliance with the law represented a rational reliance on the legal structure, and there is no need to discount this assumption. If, however, we are to proceed from the premise that the systematic influence of the law is increasing as the legal structure grows, it must also be understood how violation of the law can represent a rational reliance on legal structure.

## Traditional Notions of Rationality and the Law

Traditional jurisprudence has dealt with two categories of response to law: response by state officials and response by private persons. The concept of rational application of the law by state officials can be traced to the work of Max Weber, a late nineteenth and early twentieth-century German lawyer who ironically is more widely known among sociologists than among those in the legal profession. He distinguished 'formal' from 'substantive' rationality in the creation and application of law. 'Formal' rationality was held to exist 'to the extent that, in both substantive and procedural matters, only *unambiguous general characteristics* of the facts of the case are taken into account'. Two sub-categories of 'formal' rationality were (a) that of attaching elements of the facts to elements of the law and (b) that of logically relating elements of fact to elements of extra-legal rules, such as those of ethics or politics. 'Formal' irrationality, then, became an application of the law by an element of chance, such as an ordeal (or perhaps by jury deliberation). 'Substantive' irrationality was the application of an *ad hoc* or purely personal standard to a case. To Weber, rationality in the application of the law reached its zenith when 'formal' rationality alone became the principle by which law was applied. Under such circumstances, the terms of the law would fully determine the application of the law to any case, and state officials would automatically carry out that mandate.

Currently accepted ideas of how law can influence private persons were conceived as long ago as the eighteenth century by a group of Englishmen, including John Locke and Jeremy Bentham, and by a member of the Milanese intelligentsia, Cesare Beccaria. These 'utilitarians' believed that if 'the rational man' knew precisely how the law would apply to his conduct and if the negative sanctions imposed for violations of the law were just severe enough, 'the rational man' would be law-abiding. As Berman and Greiner summarised the position more than two centuries later, 'A general function of law in any society is that of enabling members of the society to calculate the consequences of their conduct . . .'

3

And so, for officials and for private persons alike, rationality has been held to imply literal compliance with the law's terms. If, for example, the law of New York State mandates (as it does) a life sentence for anyone selling hard narcotics, state officials acting rationally would uniformly mete out a life sentence to anyone they proved to have sold hard narcotics. Further, if the law were formally rationally applied, no rational citizen would sell hard narcotics. Legally rational actors would not do otherwise. Though some actors might try to 'rationalise' the selling of hard narcotics, the selling would nevertheless be irrational in the face of a legal proscription rationally enforced. The new jurisprudence proposed here treats legal irrationality as an empty category. All behaviour of state officials administering the law, whether licit or illicit, is assumed to be rationally responsive to the law, and all behaviour of citizens who act with an awareness that the law purports to cover their activity is likewise assumed to be rational.

## Rational Response to the Law in a New Light

Philosophers and anthropologists have treated the concept of rationality with a sense of cultural relativism practically unknown in literature or jurisprudence. To avoid the absurdity of finding the influence of the law to attenuate as the formal legal structure grows, he who interprets response to the law must bring a kind of cultural relativism to his analysis. Like ethnographers, studying cultural behaviour patterns, scholars of jurisprudence would do well to try to infer a logic by which illicit and licit behaviour patterns can be implied together by one formal legal structure.

Starting from the assumption that all recurring behaviour patterns are, in part at least, rational responses to the law, other principles of jurisprudence can be induced from the patterns of social behaviour we find around us. One set can be derived for response by officials of the state formally charged with applying the law (called 'administrators' in this book), another set for response by private persons (referred to collectively in this book as 'the general populace').

Part I of the book is an attempt to derive principles of administrators' response to formal written criminal law as found in American society. The first three chapters describe major constraints imposed on

4

administrators by the form and substance of the law. At the end of chapter 3, a strategy is outlined for optimal response within the constraints.

Chapter 4 is a case study in administration of the criminal law. Data from literature on American police decision-making are used to examine how closely the hypothetical strategy outlined in chapter 3 fits actual administrative practice. The conclusion of this examination is that application of the law by the police conforms rather well to the optimal strategy formally implied by constraints on all administrators. For better or worse, it seems fair to infer that administrators generally are constrained to favour the personal interests of some people over others, while keeping the principles by which the law is applied safe from public view.

Having reached a set of conclusions about how the structure of American formal written criminal law affects the form of rational administration of the law, consideration turns to general popular response to the law in Part II of the book. Here, a methodological problem is posed that is not confronted in Part I. The influence of formal written criminal law on administrative behaviour is manifest and direct, but most other people have little or no direct contact with the law's application. Inference of a relationship between the structure of formal written criminal law and general patterns of social action is more tenuous and difficult to make. To meet the problem, an intersocietal comparative approach is taken in chapters 5 and 6. Social phenomena in the United States are compared to those in the People's Republic of China.

The People's Republic of China is unique in being the only large, complex social system that has no comprehensive criminal code and very few formal written criminal laws at all. Those laws that do exist are relatively rarely and even then apparently capriciously applied. In China, there seems to be a predominant ideological commitment to moving away from development of what scholars of jurisprudence refer to as 'the principle of legality', a commitment antithetical to that commonly embraced in the United States.

Chapter 5 suggests that criminal law in the United States is structured to reward individual accomplishment among the general populace, while, in the People's Republic of China, criminal law is structured to reward collective accomplishment. Carried further in chapter 6, the analysis suggests that the kind of reliance on formal written criminal law characteristic of American society is uniquely suited to reinforcing inter-personal competition and distrust, and a high rate of social mobility throughout the population. It is concluded that this social character forms the dominant pattern of rational response to formal written criminal law by the American general populace.

In chapter 7 it is suggested that the pattern of popular response dictated by the form and substance of the written criminal law in the United States is a necessary and conceivably sufficient condition for the growth of crime rates in the American social system. In an important sense, the kind of formal written criminal law relied upon by Americans is an essential cause of crime itself! Rather than reducing the scope and size of the American 'crime problem', formal written criminal law actually contributes to them, for the structure of the law influences American administrators to adopt a strategy of reporting more crime. The administrators cannot hope to 'fight' crime by applying the criminal law in its American form; they are constrained instead to helping sustain relatively high rates of crime.

Many Americans express approval of a goal of at least stopping increases in, if not substantially reducing, the official rates at which crimes and criminals are found among them. The question arises as to how the law might be revised to help to achieve this end. Since Americans, unlike the Chinese, are accustomed to reliance on a large body of formal written law, it seems unrealistic to suppose that formal written criminal law could be largely eliminated in the United States. The body of the law will doubtless grow instead. Acceding to this premise, chapters 8 and 9 in Part III consist of proposals for a new kind of formal written law designed to change the American pattern of popular and administrative response to the criminal law. The proposals in chapter 8 are for incorporation of new kinds of positive incentives to social action into the substance of the law, while the proposal in chapter 9 is for incorporation of a negative incentive. These are intended to be illustrative rather than definitive of how Americans might legislate more effectively to control crime in their society.

One argument that is expected in response to the kind of change proposed in Part III is that it fails to take into account mankind's inherently aggressive and violent nature. Accepting that premise about mankind for the sake of discussion, the analysis in chapter 10 (Part IV) concludes that adoption of the type of proposal made in Part III has a reasonable chance of contributing to crime control in American society despite the human predilection.

*Origins and Methodology*

In a very real sense, this study began more than ten years ago. During a year's stay in Scandinavia, a Swedish psychologist, Magnus Hedberg, questioned the present author's definition of 'democracy' predicated on a system of laws that established and protected people's freedom to live without interference from others, and that helped to define the duty of a citizen to work for others. Hedberg characterised that definition as peculiarly American in that it spoke of freedom *from* others and of working *for* others. 'Can you conceive of a political system that represents freedom *to* do things and to work *with* others?' he asked.

Hedberg's challenge amounted to a charge of cultural naïvety. The challenge has inspired a continuing effort to discover the cultural significance of various definitions of freedom.

When one embarks on an attempt to understand the significance to persons of an abstract concept like freedom, it is hard to know where to begin. Each academic discipline has various kinds of data that bear on the problem. The point of origin of data collection is for all practical purposes a matter of chance. The 'discipline' involved in such a course of study consists of exposing oneself to as great a variety of data as possible, transcending the bounded perspective of one's culture to approach what historians typically term 'objectivity', and integrating the information these data present on the problem into an internally consistent whole.

Arbitrarily, then, the present author began with the study of foreign languages in college in order to gain tools to try to understand what people in other parts of the world with vastly different backgrounds from his own had to say on the subject of his study. An attempt to get as novel a perspective as possible on various meanings of freedom and the social orders that accompanied them led to major concentration on the language of a large number of people that seemed strangest to the author — Chinese.

The author's postgraduate legal studies took on a special significance. For one thing, they provided an opportunity to study Chinese law. The practical absence from the People's Republic of China of the

7

kind of law studied in most other law classes was fascinating. While the importance of formal written law for establishing and maintaining a social order that preserved personal freedom for the subjects of the state seemed to be a premise of American legal study, the leaders of the new China, in an effort to bring 'democracy' to 'the people' and set them free, abolished far more law than they created, and, after 1957, they seemed to be moving steadily further from reliance on a formal legal structure. Study of the logic of this strategy led eventually to chapter 5 of this book.

Experience as a student public defender and in coursework that included the standard criminal law classes and in a 'crime and society' course taught jointly by a sociologist (or criminologist) and a lawyer added a new dimension to the inquiry. How could a societal value for personal freedom be reconciled in practice with putting people in institutions and with official publication of statistics indicating that still more people should be punished or coercively treated? There seemed to be more contradictions in how people tried to be free and to keep others free than could be synthesised by Western legal scholarship.

Thus the inquiry was carried into the graduate study of sociology, where the work of ethnomethodologists and especially the philosophical foundation of ethnomethodology provided by Alfred Schutz seemed especially relevant. Though some have found the theoretical work of Schutz and Max Weber to be incompatible, their writings implied a common approach to relating disparate data on the relationship between law and preservation of personal freedom. What both these writers made clear was the importance not only of isolating the patterns of data that people produced to describe social orders and personal freedom, but of trying to infer the meaning those people ascribed to the patterns they created. If the observer were to predict which kinds of data people would produce under a new set of conditions, he or she had to base the prediction on inferences as to the motives people had in producing 'a' data under 'x' conditions, such that the same motives would lead the rational actor to produce 'b' data under 'y' conditions (as in another culture).

How are motives to be inferred in the first place? In describing the construction of an 'ideal' or 'pure type' of social action, Weber suggested an answer: the social scientist observer assumes that the motives of the actor producing data are the same as would be the observer's own were he or she in the same situation, having had the

8

same experience, as the actor. If interpretations of action are to transcend solipsism and have predictive value, one must be able to make the assumption that all people similarly situated with similar prior experience of how the social environment responds to their acts will be motivated to act in the same way. This is another way of stating that all people share a common rationality that guides their actions.

For purposes of observation and interpretation of the meaning of people's production of social data, 'experience' translates into a sequence of situations followed by response followed by situations, and so forth, that precede the latest production of data. The observer looks at the data from one situation, tries to project himself or herself into that situation, and conceives how he or she would have been motivated to respond, that is to say, what kind of data he or she would have produced under the circumstances. Then the observer checks whether this prediction corresponds to the data that the actor or actors in that situation actually produced. If the two correspond, the observer can conclude tentatively that the motives of the actors are adequately understood and can impute motives conceived by the observer to the actor or actors being observed.

However, more often than not, the two sets of data do not correspond. In scientific terms, this represents disconfirmation of a hypothesis or theory. The methodology's assumption of shared rationality does not permit the observer to conclude that the actor or actors are irrational or deviant. The observer must presume that he or she must look at prior situations or other features of the same situation to find consistency at a higher level. Ultimately, the observer must be able to account for the way in which the actor or actors conform perfectly to a norm that is logically optimally prescribed for fulfilment of *the observer's* own values.

These considerations led to the following assumptions in this study:

a) the response of all people to formal written law is based on values or motives common to each other (including the present author); and

b) the response of all people to formal written law conforms to a logically optimal strategy for reaching the goals implied by the values or motives we all share.

The essence of the research presented in this volume is to find conclusions about people's response to formal written law that are consistent with these assumptions. Since the present author values the establishment and maintenance of a social order logically suited to preserving personal freedom and values personal freedom itself, it is assumed that other people do likewise, and that their responses to the legal structure that happens to confront them are optimally suited to fulfilling these values. It is assumed that this is no more or less true of a Swedish psychologist than of any American or any Chinese.

Many of the data used are secondary. To arrive at conclusions consistent with the stated assumptions, data about features of situations and responses to them have been drawn upon that go far beyond personal capacity for direct observation. Inconsistencies arising out of one set of data, primary or secondary, have led to a search for new sources of data. The data in a single academic discipline have not sufficed for arriving at conclusions that satisfy the epistemological assumptions made, and the reader will therefore find data here from those trained variously in accounting, anthropology, biology (or medicine), economics, history, journalism, law (including juris-prudence), linguistics, philosophy, political science, psychology, social work and sociology (including criminology), with each set of data interpreted in the light of the others. It is to be hoped that the depth of the inquiry does not suffer too much from the breadth that seemed to be needed. Tentatively speaking, the conclusions finally reached do seem to meet the stated assumptions. On that basis, this research on patterns of rational response to formal written criminal law is offered to the reader.

NOTES AND REFERENCES

1. Thanks are given for permission to adapt the first part of the introduction from the present author's article, 'New conceptions of rational response to formal written law'. *Et al.* 3 (August 1974): 9—18.

# PART I

# Response to the Criminal Law by Administrators of the Criminal Law

# 1. CONSTRAINTS ON THE AMERICAN ADMINISTRATOR: MORE DETAILED LAW INCREASES DISCRETION[1]

## Introduction

Regardless of personal predilection, there are several things that the American administrator of the criminal law is constrained to do by the structure of the law he or she is to apply to persons under his or her jurisdiction. 'Administrator' is a term used here to refer to any governmental official whose primary duties are those of application of the law, including, for instance, the police, judges, trial counsel and prosecutors, court services personnel, correctional staff and parole officers and board members. Much of the literature on the activities of administrators has accepted the premises underlying the rhetoric of the formal law itself — finding fault and laying blame on administrators for somehow choosing to do wrong. Little awareness has been demonstrated of the possibility that many of the criticised actions of administrators are demanded by the form and content of the law they are given, as Part I of this book argues to be the case.

The thesis of this chapter is that the source of problems any administrator is apt to face in applying the criminal law lies in the administrator's being less guided by the terms of the law the more specifically those terms are made. Stated conversely, the more a legislator specifies the terms of the law to an administrator, the less predictable the administration of the law must become. Inversely, administration of a law will be more routine and predictable the more vague and general the terms of the law are made.

The popular conception has been that the administrators' power, particularly that of deciding whether an act is a crime and its perpetrator eligible for state 'correction', is restricted by the terms of the criminal law (including laws stated in writing in statutes and judicial

13

opinions, regulations, rules, policies and standards — both substantive and procedural). According to the stereotyped view, the law prescribes what administrators' actions are to be to an extent, beyond which the administrators legitimately exercise their private judgement or *discretion*. It is held that the more specific the terms of the law, the more limited is the extent to which administrators can exercise legitimate discretion.

In a book devoted to a discussion of discretion, Davis defines discretion more broadly:

> a public officer has discretion whenever the effective limits on his power leave him free to make a choice among possible courses of action or inaction . . . Especially important is the proposition that discretion is not limited to what is authorized or what is legal but what is within 'the effective limits on the officer's power'. This phraseology is necessary because a good deal of discretion is illegal or of questionable legality. (1969:4)

Thus Davis raises issues of administrators' compliance with the law. These issues are admittedly important to legislative control of the law's application, but they are distinct from the problem of determining what form compliant administration of the law shall take. Discussion here is limited to action of administrators that is consistent with the terms of the law — to fully legitimate official decisions as to whether acts are to be designated as crimes. To begin with, this means that the relationship between the form of the law and areas of discretion must be determined. As used here, an *area of discretion* is:

> Any basis, except uncertainty as to the credibility of evidence, in written substantive and procedural criminal laws, regulations, rules, policies and standards for a choice between designation of an act as criminal or noncriminal.

On the face of it, specification of provisions of the criminal law can serve to eliminate areas of discretion. Davis (1969:42—43) takes this position. However, as is shown in this chapter, the process of legal specification invariably multiplies the number of areas of discretion open to the administrator. Of course, if administrators tend to decide to apply the law in the same way, it can make no practical difference

14

how many areas of discretion are open to them. Hart (1961:123) seems to equate 'uncertainty' with a lack of uniformity in application of a law. If this is the case, his suggestion that specification of the law can reduce uncertainty in the law's application is open to question. As a matter of fact, as will be shown, not only do areas of discretion increase with specification of the terms of the law, but variation in the application of the law can also be expected to result.

*Implication by Substantive Criminal Law Provisions of Areas of Discretion*

Nagel (1969:664—684) has ably discussed the connection between language and the things it purports to describe. He cites the Aristotelian principle of logic that 'the same attribute cannot at the same time belong and not belong to the same object in the same respect' (1969:666). This seemingly means, for example, that someone cannot simultaneously embezzle and not embezzle, or steal and not steal what is and is not a thing which is and is not of value and is and is not of the United States, and so forth. This implies that the law could conceivably specify completely whether any conduct is or is not lawful, and so potentially eliminate ambiguities that provide areas of discretion in the law's application.

However, as Nagel points out, the qualification 'in the same respect' is fatal to the capacity of language to complete the specification of attributes of anything. Observes Nagel:

> . . . a skillful defender of the principle (that an attribute cannot at the same time belong and not belong to a subject) as an ontological truth would refuse to provide the desired stipulation (of which respect is in question). For he would recognize that if a 'respect' is first specified, it is always possible to find a way of apparently violating the principle . . . The crucial point is that in specifying both the attribute and the conditions, *the principle is employed as a criterion* for deciding whether the specification of the attribute is suitable and whether those conditions are in fact determinate. Because of the manner in which the qualification 'the same respect' is used, the principle cannot be put to a genuine test, since no

15

proposed case for testing the principle will be judged as admissible which violates the principle to be tested. In brief, conformity to the principle is the condition for a respect being 'the same respect'. (1969:667)

A provision of the United States Criminal Code headed 'Public Money, Property or Records' will be used to illustrate Nagel's point. The provision reads:

> Whoever embezzles, steals, purloins or knowingly converts to his use or the use of another, or without authority sells, conveys or disposes of any record, voucher, money, or thing of value of the United States or of any department or agency thereof, or any property made or being made under contract for the United States or any department thereof; or Whoever receives, conceals, or retains the same with intent to convert it to his use or gain, knowing it to have been embezzled, stolen, purloined or converted — Shall be fined not more than $10,000 or imprisoned not more than ten years, or both; but if the value of such property does not exceed the value of $100, he shall be fined not more than $1,000 or imprisoned not more than one year, or both. The word 'value' means face, par or market value, or cost price, either wholesale or retail, whichever is greater. (United States Code, 1948)

Stipulating that a case is in question in which all elements of a violation of the provision have been established except that of whether 'the value of such property', money orders, exceeds $100, the law does not require the exercise of discretion if, and only if, a subject, the money orders, cannot simultaneously have and not have the same attribute, a value exceeding $100. To complete the specification of conduct and preclude the exercise of discretion, the law must first specify a single respect in which the money orders and value exceeding $100 are the same. Suppose it is established that the face value of the orders is $1,200; while the value of the orders in the 'thieves' market' is $80. If these two facts can be shown to be 'in the same respect', then the exercise of discretion may not be required by the law.

If the two pieces of evidence are in the same respect, they must share a common attribute, i.e. one which at the same time does and does not belong to the same subject in the same respect. Administrators

16

of law could look for another attribute, as they often do. Here it might be evidence of the market most readily available to the defendant. Suppose, then, it is further established that the defendant knew a fence who would take the orders for $80, and that he also knew how to obtain forged validation of the orders for a small fee to cash them at face value. Suppose further he obtained the forged validation and was caught and arrested in the act of trying to cash the first money order. The question is now posed: Is this evidence in the same respect? It is in the same respect only if it shares a specified common attribute; otherwise, discretion is still a condition imposed by the law. The provision specifies that 'value' means the greater of the face and market values. But is the face value $1,200 if there is no official validation of the orders, or do the orders have no face value with a forged validation? This requires further specification. For mental exercise, the reader can provide further specification of another attribute of the value, distinguish respects in which the money orders do and do not have a value greater than $100 under the specification, further specify an attribute and so forth. Nagel's point: that language allows distinctions to be made among respects indefinitely, so that the choice of 'the same respect' is never dictated by specification of attributes. This principle, that language does not determine its own meaning, has long been accepted by semanticists (see e.g. Hayakawa, 1972).

Garfinkel (1967) would suggest that at some possibly determinate point people would simply take for granted that application of the law is determined by the law's terms. However, he has also demonstrated that what is at one point taken for granted can later be called into question (Garfinkel, 1963). The philosophy of language shows that law itself must always provide areas of discretion — areas in which any application of a provision of law can be called into question. Garfinkel indicates that administrators may choose to act as if the application of the law were determinate, though the law does not dictate that they do so. Hence, while administrators of the law may act as if the law dictated their actions, the law offers choices of action.

*Relationship between Substantive Law and Areas of Discretion*

It has been established in the preceding section that the attempt to

17

close an area of discretion of the law by the specification creates at least one new area of discretion. Further analysis reveals that such specification implies not one, but several new areas of discretion.

The simplest new legal specification will introduce a new combination of a subject and a predicate (at least of a clause and sometimes of a complete sentence). An attribute of criminal conduct under terms of the law must specify both an author of the act and the act itself. The character of the actor is embodied in the concept of criminal responsibility; the character of the act itself is embodied in the concept of social injury.

Since what is not the subject of the conduct specified in the federal statute, *not a person who* has stolen property, and/or what is not the conduct itself, *no stealing of property* has occurred, do not belong to the legally prescribed category (conduct that constitutes a person's stealing property), there are at least three different sets of evidence that can establish that the statutory provision (whoever steals property) should not be applied: evidence that a particular person was not the one who committed the act, evidence that the person is the author of the act but that what he did is not stealing property, and evidence unfounding the occurrence of stealing of property before identification of any suspect (i.e. evidence leading one to the conclusion that the stealing did not occur). Therefore, instead of one area of discretion being open that any legal attribute may simultaneously belong and not belong to a form of conduct, there are at least three.

As the federal theft statute discussed above indicates, legal provisions generally are detailed enough to specify the occurrence of more than two basic elements of conduct as a condition for the law's application. Each legal characterisation of conduct implies *at least* three unresolved questions about application of the law — three areas of discretion. Any legislative specification of the way in which any of these questions is to be resolved implies three more questions. For instance, if the term 'embezzles' is added to the statute after 'steals', then three areas of discretion are created with reference to application of the law to the case of a person who embezzles. Discretionary contingencies provided by the terms of the substantive law increase geometrically with substantive legal specifications of conduct.

Substantive criminal law provisions (i.e., those pertaining to criminal conduct) are themselves one set of standards of conduct for criminal law administrators. A legislator may also attempt to prescribe how law is to be applied by enactment of procedural law (i.e., those pertaining to the way in which a law is to be applied). However, specification of the terms of procedural law also generates areas of discretion, as illustrated in this section.

Procedural standards (or rules or policies) do not differ from the substantive law in the sense that each provision still has a subject and a predicate. Some provisions dictate conduct for officials just as the substantive law dictates it for private persons. For instance, the American Bar Association's *Standards Relating to the Prosecution and Defense Function* (1970: sec. 5.6.(a), p. 38) states in part: 'It is unprofessional conduct for a prosecutor knowingly to offer false evidence . . .' Areas of discretion are opened as to whether false evidence is offered, whether it is offered knowingly by the prosecutor (see United States Supreme Court, 1950) and whether a particular person (such as the Attorney-General in a federal case) occupies the status of prosecutor.

At least two areas of discretion are generated by a simple rule of criminal procedure with an inanimate subject, such as one stating that hearsay evidence is inadmissible at trial. One area of discretion is that of whether the subject of the sentence pertains to a particular case (e.g., of whether evidence is hearsay) and the other of whether the action stated in the predicate has occurred (e.g., whether it has been admitted at trial). This is still sufficient for geometric amplification of areas of discretion. Note also that the addition of a modifier to a simple subject or predicate, such as the adjective 'hearsay' before 'evidence', multiplies areas of discretion further. Conceivably, for example, a hearsay statement could be admitted but be so clearly irrelevant to any issue at trial that it would not be considered evidence within the rule.

Thus any specification of the way in which a crime is officially to be designated amplifies discretion. Implications may now properly be discussed of the proposition that the number of areas of discretion increases geometrically as provisions of the body of the criminal law are further specified.

19

The proposition establishes merely that there are linguistic bases upon which discretion can be exercised if sufficient information comes to an administrator's attention. By the literal terms of the law, it is invariably open to an administrator to continue to develop evidence either to the point of designating a stipulated act as a crime or to the point of deciding not to make such a designation; the terms of the law force no choice upon him.

However, a change in the number of areas of discretion is not the same as a change in quantity of discretion in Davis's (1969:43n) terms or as a change in the amount of uncertainty in the application of a legal provision in Hart's (1961:123) terms. On the face of it at least, though an area of discretion exists in the application of a provision of the law, the law can still be applied uniformly to particular cases. Though written guidelines do not dictate whether an administrator designates a stipulated act to be someone's crime, the application of the law may prove to be relatively predictable. By conforming to the predictions of others, one can say that an administrator does not *exercise* the discretion given him by the terms of the law.

How does one determine whether discretion is exercised when an area of discretion is open to use? Davis's (1969:4) definition of discretion does not facilitate such a determination. If an actor designates an act as a crime, how can one establish that 'the effective limits on his power' left him 'free to make a choice' not to do so? A person can only act in one way at a time; what he might have been 'free' to have 'chosen' to do otherwise lies in the realm of speculation. Hence, although if there were no area of discretion an administrator could not have exercised discretion, there is no way under Davis's definition of establishing whether an administrator has *exercised* discretion when an area of discretion exists.

Another approach to defining the exercise of discretion is more fruitful. Hart (1961:123) suggests that specification of a legal provision can reduce uncertainty in its application. Hart provides no support for his proposition. He also fails to provide a criterion for determining whether 'uncertainty' exists. Perhaps, though, Hart is hinting at a distinction more recently drawn from a range of literature (including Hart's) by Chambliss and Seidman (1971:75—155) — that between the 'clear cases' in which the legitimate application of the law admits of no doubt, and 'trouble cases'. The application of the law is relatively predictable in 'clear cases'; discretion characteristically is exercised in 'trouble cases'. Hence, the more 'trouble cases' that can be expected to arise in the application of a law, the greater the exercise of discretion that can be anticipated in the application of the law.

Chambliss and Seidman's examples of 'trouble cases' are noteworthy in one respect. They involve both seldom-applied legal provisions (such as those defining insanity and first-degree murder) and seldom-alleged facts (such as defendant responding to victim's request to be killed or defendant killing because he believed victim to be a witch). On the other hand, 'clear cases' involve the application of legal provisions so often applied previously that they are invested with the aura of custom or routine. A specification newly added by a legislator to control 'discretion' cannot immediately be invested with such a tradition in its application. Even if terms (such as 'embezzles') are borrowed from prior law, the terms will have to be applied in new contexts and the old meaning is lost in translation. Reliance on a new specification of the law would therefore characteristically be expected to lead to a 'trouble case'. It is not so much that new cases arise, but that what once were considered 'clear cases' for application of the law are apt to become 'trouble cases'. Therefore, not only does specification of the law generate areas of discretion, but it is also more likely than older areas of discretion to generate 'trouble cases'. Specification of the law generates new areas of discretion, *and* makes it more likely that available discretion will be exercised. New legislation tends to make administration of the criminal law less predictable than before until new customs of application develop, and the more law there is, the longer the customs take to develop. Thus, specification of the law makes it harder for administrators to claim, 'I am applying the law to this case as the law dictates'.

There is empirical evidence that administration of the law becomes more predictable where little written guidance is given administrators. A mandate that is vague to the outsider is likely to be straightforward to the practitioner. Thus, for example, Pepinsky (1972) was initially struck by the abstract vagueness of a mandate to police patrolmen to report offences, but found that the patrolmen's decisions as to whether to report offences in response to calls from a police dispatcher were practically fully predictable in an active city precinct. The language of the dispatcher — the patrolmen's first information about a possible

21

offence – was the basis of the offence-reporting decisions. Similarly, Sudnow (1965) found decisions of public defenders as to plea bargains to be straightforwardly determined by the language of arrest reports, though the law gave little guidance as to what bargains would be made. The cause of these predictable patterns of administration appears to be this: the less specific and more long-established the provisions of a law, the less the application of the provisions is apt to be challenged in a given time period. The less frequent the challenge, the more easily uniformity of administrative decision-making is established and maintained.

Two research hypotheses suggest themselves as a further test of the thesis of the discussion. First, if a number of subjects were asked to apply the law to the same case, the rate of consensus on the application should decrease as the specificity of provisions given the subjects in the area of law in question increased (i.e., the index of reliability of application would decline). Second, should legislators be asked to apply their legal provisions to the same cases as have administrators, the rate of legislative disagreement with the administrators should tend to increase with increasing specificity of provisions in the area of law in question. A supervisor (see Davis, 1969:142–161) may be in a position to account for an administrator's application of the law rather precisely in retrospect, but the more precisely a legislator tries to determine application of the law, the less precisely he is apt to do so!

And yet the feeling persists that rule-making reduces the scope of legitimate discretion. The feeling does have a rational foundation, although the rationale confuses logical justification of an application of the law with the law's logical determination of the application. Dworkin (1963:635) justifies restrictions on discretion in part by arguing that 'good reasons for judicial decisions must be *public* standards rather than *private* prejudice'. Perhaps additions to criminal law standards hide the prejudices underlying official decisions as to when and where to designate crime. Many American law students learn that their professors characteristically pay far less attention to answers to legal questions than they do to complexity and internal consistency of presentation of legal argument. As areas of discretion multiply, attention to the choice of option in each area of discretion is displaced by attention to the process of following paths from one area of discretion to the next, for, practically speaking, this becomes the only way to conceptualise the overall administrative decision as an integral whole. Preoccupation with deductive legal reasoning tends to overshadow concern for the bases of induction of the attributes of an act in question. Thus, in so far as discussion of discretion and uncertainty in the administration of criminal law reflect concern over whether provisions of the law *appear* to account for administrative action, specification of the law may be advocated to control discretion. Appearances, however, are deceptive.

*Conclusion*

Even assuming that administrators of the criminal law adhere 'strictly' to the law's terms, specification of the law does not tend to determine what the administrators do but to present them with options as to courses of action to follow. Each new provision adds more than one option to the administrator's repertoire. Paradoxically, then, attempts to move toward determination of administration of the law give the administrator wider legitimate latitude for varying application of the law.

This is not to say that legal specification cannot be used to engineer changes of particular kinds in the administration of criminal justice. Observers of criminal justice administration are even apt to be led by legal specification to conclude that the administration is tending toward standardisation. Specification of the law can divert attention from the ways in which the law is applied to various cases, thereby helping to increase the scope of unchallenged variation in the law's application. In Dworkin's (1963:635) terms, the appearance of adherence to public principle is strengthened as the points for exercise of private prejudice multiply. Ironically, the more precisely the criminal law appears to prescribe its own application, the less precisely it does so.

Herein lies the basic dilemma posed to the American administrator of the criminal law. As the body of American criminal law grows in scope and detail, the administrator is called upon to do his best to maintain the appearance of adherence to public principle with less and less guidance from the terms of the law themselves. The administrator is constrained by the structure of the law to depend increasingly on extra-legal strategies for avoiding criticism about how the law is applied.

## NOTES

1. Thanks are given for permission to adapt this chapter from the present author's article, 'Generation of discretion by specification of the criminal law'. *International Journal of Criminology and Penology*, 3 (May 1975): 111–121.

## REFERENCES

American Bar Association. 1970. *Standards Relating to the Prosecution and Defense Function*. Chicago: American Bar Association.

Chambliss, William J. and Robert B. Seidman. 1971. *Law, Order, and Power*. Reading, Mass.: Addison-Wesley Publishing Co.

Davis, Kenneth Culp. 1969. *Discretionary Justice: A Preliminary Inquiry*. Baton Rouge, Louisiana: Louisiana State University Press.

Dworkin, Ronald. 1963. 'Symposium: philosophy of law-judicial discretion'. *Journal of Philosophy*, 60 (26 September): 624–638.

Garfinkel, Harold. 1963. 'A conception of, and experiments with "trust" as a condition of stable concerted actions', in O. J. Harvey (ed.), *Motivation and Social Interaction: Cognitive Determinants*, pp. 187–238. New York: Ronald Press Company.

Garfinkel, Harold. 1967. *Studies in Ethnomethodology*. Englewood Cliffs, New Jersey: Prentice-Hall, Inc.

Hart, H. L. A. 1961. *The Concept of Law*. Oxford, England: Clarendon Press.

Hayakawa, Samuel I. 1972. *Language in Thought and Action*. New York: Harcourt Brace Jovanovich, Inc. (3rd edn).

Nagel, Ernest. 1969. 'Language without ontology', in Thomas M. Olshewsky (ed.), *Problems in the Philosophy of Language*, pp. 664–684. New York: Holt, Rinehart and Winston, Inc.

Pepinsky, Harold E. 1972. *Police Decisions to Report Offenses*. Philadelphia: University of Pennsylvania (dissertation).

Sudnow, David. 1965. 'Normal Crimes: Sociological Features of the Penal Code in a Public Defenders Office'. *Social Problems*, 12 (Winter):255–276.

United States Code. 1948. U. S. C., title 18, sec. 641.

United States Supreme Court. 1950. *Nabue v. Illinois*. 360 U.S. 264.

## 2.  CONSTRAINTS ON THE AMERICAN ADMINISTRATOR: THE LAW IMPOSES SOCIAL BIAS[1]

*Introduction*

This chapter describes another major constraint imposed on administrators by the inherent substance of the criminal law. Marx (e.g. 1963:38), Robison (1936), Quinney (1974), and Chambliss (1975), among many, many others, have noted the socio-economic bias pervasive in the application of the law. But could American criminal law be applied in an unbiased way if administrators desired to do so? If it can be shown that the bias inheres in the form of the law itself, it is unnecessary to demonstrate that the application of the criminal law favours the interests of identifiable socio-economic status groups, such as one that might be termed 'the bourgeoisie', in order to prove that the application of the law is socio-economically biased. As lawyers might put it, any statement that the law is an instrument of a particular group (which also might be identified as 'the capitalists') becomes *dictum*; it is not essential to a determination that the application of the criminal law is inevitably socio-economically biased.

The bias does indeed inhere in a particular element of the structure of American law: the way the law defines social injury. The essential object of the application of the criminal law is to react to legally defined social injury. By assumption, any social injury defined by the criminal law has one fundamental characteristic: the injury is a denial by one or more persons of another or others' future access to use of a resource of actual or potential value to the user. This resource may be a part or the whole of a person's body (as covered by crimes against the person) or what is known as real or personal property (as covered by crimes against property). A measure of guarantee by the terms of the law to future access to the resource is called a *right*; hence, by

25

definition, a crime is a person or person's denial of a right or rights of another or others (including persons represented collectively by a corporation or the state), provided that denial is explicitly declared in a criminal statute to be wrongful.

The way the law defines social injury leads to three difficulties. First, the assumption of social injury resulting from a legally proscribed act is apt in many cases to be demonstrably problematic. Second, even if the injury can be shown to result from the act, it is often impossible to demonstrate adequately that a particular person or persons have caused legally proscribed social injury. Third, even in any case in which it can be adequately demonstrated that a person or persons have acted so as to cause a legally proscribed social injury, it can equally well be argued that social injury would have resulted from their failure so to act, in the form of deprivation of life, liberty or property. In so far as the law provides for the negative sanction of one social injury, it implicitly provides for the positive sanction of another. Thus, application of the law by an administrator must either be unresponsive to a social injury or represent the favouring of social injury to one or more persons over social injury to another or others, a form of socio-economic bias.

An argument between Edwin Sutherland, a sociologist, and Paul Tappan, a lawyer, in the mid-1940s, provides a basis for addressing the issues of how these difficulties inevitably arise under the kind of system of written criminal law found in the United States. These adversaries of a sort shared a common assumption — that if the term 'crime' were properly defined with reference to the terms of the written law, each of the three difficulties would be overcome. The meaning of 'social injury' would be clear to the administrator of the law; the law could be applied unproblematically as a response to this 'social injury'; and the application of the law could be without socio-economic bias (or, in Tappan's view, already was so applied). However, a close examination of their argument reveals that the assumption they shared is fundamentally open to question and revision.

*Terms of the Sutherland—Tappan Argument*

Sutherland opened his statement of position as to how crime should be

26

defined in his Presidential Address to the American Sociological Association in 1939. He wrote:

> The thesis of this paper is that the conception and explanation of crime which have just been described are misleading and incorrect, that crime is, in fact, not closely correlated with poverty, and that an adequate explanation of criminal behavior must proceed along different lines. The conventional explanations are invalid principally because they are derived from biased samples. The samples are biased in that they have not included vast areas of criminal behavior of persons not in the lower class. One of these neglected areas is the criminal behavior of business and professional men, which will be analyzed in this paper (1940:1).

In other words, Sutherland agreed that a distinctive social problem was posed by those who committed crimes and those who responded to the crimes. He saw crime, a 'legally defined social injury' for which a 'penal sanction' was provided, as a conceptually unitary phenomenon against which a society needed to protect itself (1945:132–133; later published in his book, see 1961:31–33). What bothered him was that because of a class bias in the previous definition of the phenomenon, persons of a higher socio-economic status often committed crimes with impunity. As a matter of justice, in the sense discussed by Hart (1961:153–163) that like cases be treated alike, Sutherland asked that white-collar crime be more attended to in order to remove the class bias inherent in previous criminological research. In reality, Sutherland's definition of white-collar crime was an extension of the generic definition of crime.

Opposition to the redefinition of crime has generally argued that the redefinition is too broad. Tappan (1947) typifies such opposition by arguing that a crime exists for purposes of research or other social response only when it is that for which a defendant is prosecuted and convicted. Only then, claims Tappan, are we justified in claiming the occurrence of a crime to be a fact.

27

Provision of a 'penal sanction' is at the heart of Sutherland's definition. Sutherland argues that the provision of an injunction (court-ordered action or inaction), treble damages or a stipulation (administrative agreement to do something) as relief from the injury caused by an act constitutes provision of a penal sanction. In the case of an injunction, this is because failure to obey its terms is in turn punishable by fine and/or imprisonment for contempt of court. Treble damages are held to be a punishment equivalent to a fine. A regulatory stipulation not followed may lead to a cease and desist order. Failure to obey the cease and desist order can lead to the granting of an injunction, and so on. In Sutherland's view, if a course of action can ultimately and legally lead the actor to jail or to have to pay more than the damage he is assessed to have caused, the law provides a penal sanction.

Thus construed, a simple breach of a business or professional contract is a white-collar crime, as is negligence in carrying out one's business or profession. A plaintiff may sue for the breach or the negligence in a civil court. If the court or jury finds for the plaintiff, the court customarily will make the defendant pay court costs. This is distinguished from payment of damages caused by the breach. Payment of costs, in other words, represents payment for a social injury greater than that caused to the defendant. As a social cost the defendant pays for the injury he has done; court costs fit Sutherland's notion of a penal sanction. Sutherland's definition thus effectively obliterates the distinction between civil and criminal wrongs.

Sutherland is conceptually safe in not distinguishing civil from criminal wrongs, as Tappan (1947) argues he must. The two categories do not differentiate wrongs by seriousness. The crime of embezzlement of a few thousand dollars from a large corporation, for example, would hardly be considered more serious than a company's violating a contract by carelessly delaying the shipping of badly needed equipment which cost its buyer tens of thousands of dollars in lost time.

Sutherland maintains that white-collar crimes can occur without court findings of wrongful conduct. However, even if he were to accept Tappan's view that his definition should require a court finding of wrongdoing, criminal and civil wrongs would not be significantly distinguishable. The difference in formal burden of proof required in civil and criminal proceedings is in practice illusory. Commonly, as the present author has observed directly and had corroborated by other practitioners, the judge or jury weighing the facts in a criminal case apparently begins with a presumption that the defendant is guilty or he would not be in court. This generally renders meaningless the formal requirement of proof of guilt beyond a reasonable doubt. Plea bargaining leads to guilty pleas in most cases, and so criminal defendants are usually not even tried. Sudnow (1965) found that the group of public defenders he studied based their bargaining on their own practically universal presumption of their defendant's guilt, concluding that trials would be a waste of time. Tappan's (1947) position fails of adequate support, for in most cases convictions of crime are not founded on having established guilt beyond a reasonable doubt.

From this author's limited experience and from talking with other attorneys, it would appear that, if anything, civil liability is typically founded on a more exacting burden of proof in practice than is criminal liability. The requirement of proof by a preponderance of the evidence would appear to be more rigidly adhered to than the mythical requirement of proof beyond a reasonable doubt. A form of bargaining takes place in most civil cases too, for they are generally settled out of court. However, it is standard practice for the civil defendant not to acknowledge liability and in fact to be released from all claims of liability to the plaintiff in exchange for his or her payment. Thus, if anything, there is greater reason to believe that a finding of civil liability demonstrates wrongdoing than to believe that a criminal conviction does so. If statutory criminal offences committed by business and professional people in the course of their work are to be considered white-collar crimes, it is appropriate to attach the same label to torts and breaches of contract committed by these people in their work. It begins to appear that elimination of socio-economic bias from the American concept of crime would require many acts which have previously been considered 'mere' civil wrongs to be considered crimes as well.

*'Legally Defined Social Injury' in Sutherland's Definition*

The words 'social injury' in this part of Sutherland's definition may simply be read as 'act'. Sutherland does not allow for the possibility that any act, legally defined with a penal sanction provided, is not a social injury. This assumption is highly problematic. Statutory crimes may be created without adequate evidence that a social injury is stated. The American electric company conspiracy cases of 1961 illustrate the point. (The following account of the cases is drawn from Geis, 1967, and Smith, 1961.)

In 1961, twenty-nine corporations (electric companies) and forty-five individuals were tried and convicted of anti-trust violations under the Sherman Act (United States Code, 1958). Fines were imposed and seven of the individual defendants, including a vice-president of General Electric, received thirty-day jail sentences. The defendants' crime was to arrange whose bid would be low and what the amount of the bid would be before bidding for the sale of heavy electric equipment. The bids were allocated so that each participating corporation would receive a fixed percentage of the market.

The injury said to be caused by such an arrangement is three-fold — a poorer quality product, less efficient production and higher prices to the buyers. However, these phenomena cannot be shown to result from a price-fixing arrangement.

From the point of view of economic theory, the injury caused by price-fixing is shown by models contrasting oligopolistic or monopolistic markets to competitive ones. The problem with this comparison is that a competitive market as an abstraction cannot exist as a reality. The perfect competition model assumes that there are enough suppliers for no one of them to be able to affect prices, that each of the suppliers has unlimited immediate access to all resources needed for production and distribution, that the resources can be obtained and used by all suppliers at equal, invariate cost, that cost-accounting systems are invariate among suppliers, that the cost-accounting system used shows the true cost of production and distribution and that the quality of the product is unidimensional and invariate among all suppliers. The assumptions are all too easily not met in real life. In producing heavy electric equipment, for instance, there may not be immediate access to steel during periodic shortages. Not all producers of the equipment can be equally close to producers of steel at lowest available cost. Variations in cost-accounting systems are legion, such as the difference between determining cost of a product shipped from inventory on a last-in-first-out method and on a first-in-first-out method. These methods are apt to yield different costs, while neither can be shown to be *the* right approach. Finally, advertising has taught us the vagaries of assessing the quality of a product. A supplier will naturally try to establish that his product differs from others in a way that makes it of the higher quality, and the criteria for quality can be varied to suit the supplier's product. Hence, economic modelling has no adequate way of assessing the cost to the buyer or the supplier of development of an oligopolistic or of a monopolistic market.

From an empirical point of view also, it is practically impossible to establish that harm is caused by price-fixing. Damages against the electric companies were established by comparing prices during the activity of the conspiracy to prices during a period when the conspiracy had broken down. However, the price cuts were in some measure at least a product (and a cause) of movement out of the conspiracy. These price levels do not establish what prices would have been had there been no conspiracy in the first place. In fact, to compare price levels adequately would require the simultaneous existence in the same economy of two markets for the same product with sellers and buyers having the same resources in each — one market with a price-fixing conspiracy and the other without: a situation one cannot hope to find.

As a matter of fact, the electric company conspiracies retained a strong element of competition, suggesting in another way that elements of competition on the one hand and of oligopoly and monopoly on the other in reality interact instead of acting by themselves. The electric companies fought over market shares and price levels. Demonstrably, there was considerable competition over the percentage of bids allocated to each company. The companies that were able to make the heavy electric equipment at the lowest cost could have competed within the price-fixing arrangement to have prices set at a low enough level for the less efficient producers to have to serve portions of the market at less than cost. The more efficient producers would then have had an advantage over their less efficient brethren in serving the more costly portions of the market. This would have strengthened the bargaining position of the more efficient producers in negotiations over allocation of market shares. The level of movement for competitive advantage was most forcefully demonstrated in the two periods in which electric companies underbid each other in violation of the terms of the conspiracy, and the conspiracy fell apart. From an empirical stand-point, then, price-fixing arrangements would appear to involve the same pressures for low prices and efficient production as does more manifest competition. Price-fixing, a legally defined act with a penal sanction attached, has not been shown to constitute a social injury, and no such evidence suggests itself for further consideration.

Conversely, a social injury committed in the course of business or professional activity may not be legally defined (let alone not have a penal sanction provided). For example, automobile exhaust unleashed wilfully by a driver contributes substantially to air pollution. In this sense the driver is committing a social injury, though the act of releasing exhaust fumes is not in and of itself legally defined as a crime in any sense. One might consider the decision of a businessman to use trucks instead of trains to move his product a white-collar crime because of the greater air pollution given off by the trucks, but under American law, the doing of this kind of social injury cannot be considered a crime. If all acts causing social injury are to be treated equitably, such treatment cannot be limited to acts proscribed by American criminal law.

### Problems of Applying Sutherland's Definition

There are practical as well as conceptual problems with Sutherland's attempt to remove socio-economic bias from the definition of crime within the context of American law. Groves's (1958) study of income-tax compliance by residential landlords (excluding corporations) in a Wisconsin city illustrates the point. It appears to be the most careful attempt to date to locate and describe a kind of white-collar crime. Groves found what to him were some clear cases of tax evasion. Twenty-three multiple-unit landlords who indicated in interviews that they had an average rental income of slightly over $1,000 had not filed state returns. It is, however, possible that exemptions and eligibility for reporting income jointly with spouses lowered their income sufficiently for them not to be legally required to file returns. For the few (eight) multiple-unit landlords who filed returns but reported no rental income (who again reported to interviewers an average income slightly in excess of $1,000), there is no indication that the interview estimates of income took account of vacancies or delinquent rent payments. Depending on how the interviewers presented themselves, the landlords might have felt moved to exaggerate the income they received to demonstrate business acumen. It is also possible that for these landlords rental expenses exceeded income. In such a case the landlords would be guilty of filing improper returns, but not necessarily of tax evasion.

Groves purportedly showed that those landlords reporting rental income over-reported their expenses by approximately 10 per cent, thereby evading taxes in yet another way. This finding was based primarily on a comparison of reported expenses with estate agents' estimates as to what expenses should be (i.e., about 50 per cent of gross rent whatever the type of structure). However, estate agents (or 'realtors' in American parlance), who are in the business of selling rental property, might plausibly be expected to tend to underestimate the expenses their buyers would incur. Here again, evasion by landlords is not adequately established.

Similar criticisms could be made of the tenability of each of Groves's findings. Even this incomplete summary highlights the problems one encounters in a field of study defined by a particular and yet various set of acts. One hundred and fifty years of attempts validly to measure the occurrence of crime in general have demonstrated the futility of basing the study of any area of crime on adequate knowledge of the occurrence of most categories of legally proscribed acts (see Pepinsky, 1972:1—36). The very decision that an offence has occurred is still a complex, socially negotiated, largely unexplained process. It remains a formidable challenge to move from the abstract notion that legally proscribed acts occur to a set of adequately resolvable issues about that abstraction. Sutherland's definition fails to meet the challenge, and that task remains also for someone who would reconceptualise the subject-matter of a field of white-collar crime.

Conceptually, also, Tappan's argument that a court finding of guilt should be the operational element of the definition of white-collar crime rests on weak ground. Even in those few cases in which a jury 'determines' the fact of guilt or innocence, our faith in the determination has no more rational foundation than that of some of our predecessors in trial by ordeal (see Aubert, 1959, and Garfinkel, 1956). Indeed, protection of the secrecy of jury deliberations is plausibly explained in part as a protection of the sanctity of the myth of the infallibility of 'twelve good men and true'. While adherence to Tappan's definition would protect those not adjudicated guilty of crime, it would

33

also lend unwarranted credence to the stigma attached to convicted offenders; the latter would be the victims of Tappan's definition. In so far as Sutherland's definition would lead us to accept the greater likelihood of anyone's culpability and therefore stigmatise any white-collar criminal with less vigour than we would be inclined to do under Tappan's conception of crime, less harm would be apt to result from the use of Sutherland's definition than Tappan's reformulation. Sutherland's operational definition is thus the more acceptable of two definitions inadequate to the task of removing socio-economic bias from the application of the criminal law. Adoption of either definition as a principle of application of the law by the administrator, let alone the social scientist, would be (and is, as revealed in descriptions of police decision-making in chapter 4), a source of considerable frustration to an attempt to render equal treatment under law.

### Guidelines for a Reformulation of Sutherland's Definition

A reformulation of Sutherland's attempt to define social injury without socio-economic bias should avoid the three pitfalls described above. It should not make a spurious attempt to distinguish the commission of criminal from that of civil injury. It should not rest on the assumption that legal proscriptions describe a unitary set of phenomena. And it should not proscribe unascertainable behaviour.

Essentially, any white-collar crime is a challenge to an alleged appropriation of another's resources. A finding of tax evasion, for example, implies that resources of the government have been withheld by the taxpayer for his own use. Price-fixing is deemed criminal because presumably it enables the seller either to obtain some purchase money from the buyer or to retain control of the resources that would pass to the buyer as greater quality of the product he buys for his money. By failing to exercise legally prescribed precautions in controlling some emissions, an industry arguably uses air that has been a resource of others.

This suggests that white-collar crime is legally defined after all. The legal owner is one whose right to use of the property is superior. The rightful owner may be the one who lost the use or the one who gained it. If the one who successfully appropriates the use has a superior legal right, his act is legitimate. If this right is inferior, he has committed a crime. In a tautologous sense Sutherland was correct. Crimes are socially injurious because the law declares them to be so.

A number of social analysts, such as Marx (see, e.g., 1963) and Quinney (1970:43—97), have pointed out the weakness of the assumption that law discriminates socially injurious preferences in use of property from non-injurious preferences. As Hart (1961:155) observes in discussing justice under law, justice is relative to the respect in which 'like cases are treated alike and different cases treated differently'. The criteria that separate socially injurious preferences from non-injurious preferences are not just in themselves; they are artifacts of social power. One of the devices that can be used to secure the use of property is to influence legislatures and courts to decree that one's use is superior to another's. When an employee is convicted of embezzlement and ordered to make restitution, it affirms the legitimacy of the employer's priority over the employee in determining how the funds shall be used. If the government that makes that decree is overthrown in a revolution, the employee may be able to use the power of the new government to make the employer surrender the funds to him. If one eliminates the socio-economic bias inherent in use preference, the character of the injury to either party in not having the use of the funds must be considered essentially the same. If the parties want to use the funds in different ways, there is a social injury of essentially the same type regardless of which party prevails. To say that there is a higher social interest in maintaining one's ordering of property rights and that frustration of such an interest is a legally recognised injury implies that the interests of those similarly situated to the claimant have an inherent moral superiority over the interests of those similarly situated to the 'frustrator'. Thus, acceptance of legal definitions of ownership would represent an acceptance of some kind of socio-economic bias that Sutherland sought to avoid by his redefinition, however the bias was ordered by the law. One class of persons would be held to deserve to have resources in preference to others. A reformulation of Sutherland's definition that endorses no socio-economic bias would have to equate the position of the embezzler with that of his employer. Each causes equal social injury if he gets use of the funds in dispute. Thus, while law may be an instrument to challenge another's use of private property, the law does not define the character of the use but instead the character of the challenge. An absence of socio-economic bias dictates that the injury represented by the use be considered equivalent whenever there is a challenge regardless of whether law is an instrument of challenge. The challenger may be assumed to be indicating that he or his client wants the use of the property enjoyed by the current user. Uniformly, then, a social injury caused by those called white-collar criminals, like other criminals, is to deprive others of the use of private property by their own hegemony. For want of a better term, this deprivation as it is alleged to occur will be referred to as 'appropriation'.

## The Reformulation

Appropriation can include many acts other than those that have been considered white-collar crimes. Anything called a crime against private property would come under the rubric of appropriation. Appropriation would cover a sale of a product to a customer who expresses the belief that the quality of the product is less than he thought he or she paid for. Failure of a government to accept a producer's request to amend a defence contract because of allegedly previously unforeseen expenses would be appropriation. Note that the definition is already limited in its application. An unchallenged use of private property is not appropriation, and appropriation cannot be applied to use of other than private property.

Since the definition of appropriation is extra-legal, the definition of private property for these purposes is necessarily also extra-legal. Private property here refers *either* to a resource that the user attempts to deny to others' use on any basis other than immediate personal need for his or her own use, *or* to a resource (such as life) that the user so alters as to preclude a certain future use of the resource by others. A personal need is immediate if use of the resource is either ongoing or projected to begin before another's continuous use might reasonably be expected to terminate. Even state property may be considered private property under this definition.

This definition of private property is similar to Marx's (see Marx, 1963:137–167), but does not proceed from an analysis of the relation of people to labour. What distinguishes private property from other resources is a claim of power to deprive others of its future use. For

36

instance, if Mr Smith is vacuuming his house when Mr Jones asks for the vacuum cleaner, Mr Smith's refusal to relinquish the cleaner until the vacuuming is completed does not give the cleaner the character of private property (ownership of which may be at issue). If, however, Mr Smith refuses to relinquish the cleaner because he plans to use it in a few days, or if Mr Smith smashes the vacuum cleaner to pieces, the cleaner is private property and refusal to relinquish its use, if challenged, is appropriation. Where resources are made available to all who would use them — a collective use confirmed by an absence of any challenge — such resource is also presumed not to have the character of private property.

Conceptually, appropriation is the kind of social injury underlying all American legal definitions of crime, whether the appropriation be that of bodily resources (crimes against the person) or of extra-bodily resources (crimes against property). However, to eliminate class distinctions in the definition of social injury, the concept of appropriation far transcends the provisions of American law, both criminal and civil. The logic of the problem that led Sutherland to define white-collar crime as a social problem leads to the recognition of a social problem that only incidentally coincides with crime in any form.

*Application of the Reformulation*

Recall that the chief problem as regards practical use of Sutherland's definition was that of the impossibility of deciding whether a violation of law had 'actually' occurred. A comparable problem does not arise in the operationalisation of the concept of appropriation. Appropriation is deemed to exist by virtue of any challenge thereto, provided the challenge is by someone who claims that he or she, or someone in whose favour he or she speaks, should have or should have had use of what the challenge characterises as property. The appropriation exists by virtue of the challenge. Whether the use of private property actually occurred may remain problematic. This latter question could conceivably (if inadequately) be explored in an investigation of factors associated with appropriation, but its answer is not required to define the scope of the social problem. The challenge in itself implies the existence of the institution of private property in a society, and that alone is undoubtedly a sufficient as well as a necessary condition for contention over the use of the property. Furthermore, the accusation in the challenge presents social conflict in itself – a social injury calling for response whether or not there is truth in the allegation. This is not a new observation. The 2,000-year-old dynastic order in China was built on a recognition that one person's accusation of another necessarily represents social conflict. The Chinese made this postulate the foundation of their legal system (see Van der Sprenkel, 1962:29). The definition of appropriation implies recognition of a time-honoured principle of what constitutes a social problem.

In the American context at least, the study of that ever-so-elusive crime in general and white-collar crime in particular, and of their treatment, has been founded on an unfulfillable promise. Violations of criminal law, begins the promise, are what disrupt the harmonious coexistence of society's members. By locating the conditions that lead to crime and changing them to eliminate the phenomenon, continues the promise, society's members will live in peaceful, happy harmony. By acting against crime conscientiously, concludes the promise, we may not eliminate the causes of interpersonal strife but at least interpersonal conflict will be controlled and thereby reduced.

An analysis of Sutherland's and of Tappan's definitions of crime shows how tenuous the promise is. The substantive provisions of the law are just as apt to defend social injury as to react against it. In Sutherland's terms, a strict application of penal sanctions would likely punish most, if not all, of society's members repeatedly. And in the 'discovery' of white-collar crime, given the vagaries of operationalisation of the term, the socially powerful few could be expected amorally to prevail. The social scientist, as he thus delimits a field of inquiry, may socially dictate the categories by which one man's claim of injury is given higher status than another's, while in a paradoxical sense one man's righting of a wrong is another's wronging of a right. As Sutherland was undoubtedly moved to isolate and weaken one source of social conflict and inequity, he sowed the seeds of another source to grow additional conflict in its place.

This failing of Sutherland's definition is revealed by its conceptual and operational inadequacies. Where a conceptual inadequacy is found to exist, it is a sign that acceptance of the conceptualisation is a manifest threat to the interests of some who fear the consequences of its social acceptance. For example, those who can imagine that what a legislature proscribes might not be a social injury may be imagining that they might be punished legally for what to them is an innocuous act they foresee carrying out. Where an operational inadequacy is found to exist (in the field of sociology at least), it is apt to be because the finder fears the consequences for himself of being (or not being, as the case may be) associated with a phenomenon in a way he cannot foresee. What precautions, for example, can an academician take to avoid being branded a chronic thief for taking writing supplies from his university employer? (Professor Sutherland was apparently not overly alarmed at this prospect.)

Our conceptualisation of any field of research and action concerned with social problems necessarily implies an ideological perspective on the problem. A recognition that one man's defence against appropriation may itself be another's appropriation requires us to make an ideological choice. Are we going to define the field in such a way as to give one person's interests a higher status than those of his or her adversary?

The definition of appropriation obviates the necessity for ranking injuries. Though the injury represented by a challenge to appropriation is assumed to be real, the role of the appropriator in creating the injury is held to be problematic. Indeed, when the remedy of the victim of the appropriation is likely to result in the appropriation of resources of his alleged 'offender', deprivation of the resources of the appropriator can scarcely be seen as a viable strategy to reduce the incidence of appropriation in the society. The kinds of remedy prescribed for appropriation by American law are liable to be challenged as appropriations in their own right. Alleviation of the problem of appropriation would require that the question of what social conditions are responsible for appropriation-based conflict replaces the question of who is responsible; personal responsibility attaches to those who would change these conditions rather than to those who happen to be labelled 'appropriators'.

There are hints as to some social conditions that might be related to the incidence of appropriation in a society. To begin with, appropriation presupposes the institution of private property. There might be some societies like that of the jungle people depicted by Henry (1964) in which there is apparently no such institution and therefore no basis for a challenge to appropriation. More commonplace would be particular settings in complex societies in which the institution did not

39

exist, as might, for example, be the case with the food in the refrigerator for some families. Other distinctions between these settings and those in which appropriation occurred might provide clues as to how the institution of private property might be eliminated along with the appropriation that accompanied the institution, if such were deemed desirable.

A challenge to appropriation could reflect an ordering on one alone of two distinct concerns: that an alleged use of private property should change hands (representing implicit acceptance of appropriation as a way of life) or that the character of the resources allegedly used could be changed so that they were no longer private property at all. Where the challenge to appropriation was founded on a challenge to the institution of private property itself, as in collectivisation of farming resources in the People's Republic of China, a condition for reducing appropriation might already exist that would bear studying and possible establishment elsewhere.

One fundamental hypothesis well worth testing is that the rate of appropriation in a social setting cannot be reduced so long as those challenging it accept the institution of private property. This was Marx's assertion (see Marx, 1963:152—167). It would appear that the acceptance of the institution of private property has several concomitants, including those described below in chapter 7.

One concomitant would seem to be acceptance of social status differentiation (see Marx, 1963:3—32). The antithesis of this acceptance is not, incidentally, a belief that all men are exactly alike. It is the belief that the sum of any man's characteristics and talents is of a social worth exactly the same as any other man's, and therefore that the two different people deserve equal respect, admiration and other social reward. Acceptance of social status differentiation implies acceptance of the categorisation of people, for instance, as deviants, white-collar criminals or appropriators, rather than limiting classification to acts or social conditions. Such acceptance could well imply the casting of oneself as deserving of exclusive use of private property because one is a victim of appropriation. Possibly, also, an investment in a system of social status differentiation could support appropriation as a means of describing and maintaining other status boundaries.

Acceptance of individualism is another possible concomitant of acceptance of exploitation and of the institution of private property (see Bonger, 1969; Marx 1963:3—32; Schur, 1968:186). However, de

Tocqueville (1945:136–138) suggests that this is true only when the foundations of ascribed status have been implied away by democratic revolutions. Individualism is expressed in the norm that a man's first duty is to himself and that others must fend for themselves (see de Tocqueville, 1945:104–106). Individualism would seem to present a climate conducive to the incidence of appropriation (such that challenges are responses to the perceived antagonism of others to the self-interest that the challenger aims to protect).

At the turn of this century, a French sociologist, Emile Durkheim (in English translation, 1933), discussed the way in which the form of law would be transformed as societies become modern, complex, and subject to division of labour. He foresaw that penal law would be displaced by restitutive law, a minimal body of law designed to ensure that voluntary exchanges of property were carried out fairly. The law would serve to reinforce economic cooperation among groups of people, to secure common principles of action which lent solidarity to contractual relationships. Durkheim took for granted a common definition of what would constitute equitable exchange of property, and his forecast has fallen with this premise. In the United States, since a positive cultural value is placed on improving the value of one's property holdings relative to those of others, there is a widespread interest not merely in sharing gain with others in a process of equitable exchange, but in getting ahead at others' expense. The cultural value placed on economic aggrandizement at a net cost to others lends incentive to trying to engineer the definition of property value and of property rights to personal advantage. Since this concern transcends that of equitable access to needed resources, reaching to concern for substantiating claims to comparatively larger shares of private property in the social system, the 'repressive law' of which Durkheim spoke has not tended to wither away with increasing division of labour. The body of such law, known usually as 'criminal law', has instead expanded. And administrators have been called upon to apply the law (with an inevitable socio-economic bias) ever more widely.

A connection begins to emerge between constraints imposed on administrators of the criminal law and living conditions among the general populace. Extended analysis of this connection will be saved for Part II of this book. For now, let us return to the plight of the administrators themselves.

## Conclusion

Administrators of American criminal law are in a bind of a sort. To apply the law is to favour the property interests of some people over others. There is no way for administrators to react against appropriation save with socio-economic bias.

Social policy that can be expected to reduce the overall rate of social injury in a social system cannot simply involve decisions that one kind of injury is preferable to another, for the net incidence of social injury remains constant regardless of who is deemed victim and who perpetrator. Moreover, since there has been shown to be an inertia in the demand for hegemony over private property once the demand has been institutionalised in a social system (see Veblen, 1899), we can expect an increase in the rate of social injury without setting social forces against the phenomenon. An increased rate of application of a growing body of criminal law, as reflected in official statistics, is apparently symptomatic of the increasing rate of social injury, though not necessarily a cause of it. This is reminiscent of the almost two-millennia-old observation of a Roman historian and statesman that the growth of written law characteristically occurred after people 'began to throw off equality', and coincided with widespread corruption (Tacitus, 1964: 59—60). The structure of American criminal law constrains administrators to help to sustain the rate of social injury regardless of personal disposition to oppose the injury. The administrator who applies the criminal law can in so doing choose *which* social injury he or she will accept, but cannot choose to reject social injury altogether. The administrator does not share the freedom of the social scientist to reconceptualise his or her task. A central issue facing the administrator is to decide how to select some injuries for approval over others.

NOTES

1. Thanks are given for permission to adapt this chapter from the author's article, 'From white-collar crime to exploitation: redefinition of a field'. *Journal of Criminal Law and Criminology*, 65 (June 1974):225—233. Reprinted by special permission of the *Journal of Criminal Law and Criminology*, Copyright © 1974 by Northwestern University School of Law, Vol. 65, No. 2.

# REFERENCES

Aubert, Vilhelm. 1959. 'Chance in social affairs'. *Inquiry*, 2 (Spring):1–24.

Bonger, Willem. 1969. *Criminality and Economic Conditions*. Bloomington: Indiana University Press.

Chambliss, William J. 1975. 'Toward a political economy of crime'. *Theory and Society*, 2 (Summer):149–181.

Durkheim, Emile (George Simpson, trans.) 1933. *The Division of Law in Society*. London: Collier-Macmillan Ltd.

Garfinkel, Harold. 1956. 'Conditions of successful degradation ceremonies'. *American Journal of Sociology*, 61 (March):420–424.

Geis, Gilbert. 1967. 'The heavy electrical equipment anti-trust cases of 1961', in Marshall B. Clinard and Richard Quinney (eds), *Criminal Behavior Systems*, pp. 139–151. New York: Holt, Rinehart and Winston.

Groves, Harold M. 1958. 'An empirical study of income-tax compliance'. *National Tax Journal*, 11 (December):241–301.

Hart, H. L. A. 1961. *The Concept of Law*. Oxford, England: Clarendon Press.

Henry, Jules. 1964. *The Jungle People: A Kaingang Tribe of the Highlands of Brazil*. New York: Vintage Books.

Marx, Karl (T. B. Bottomore, ed. and trans.) 1963. *Karl Marx: Early Writings*. New York: McGraw-Hill Book Company.

Pepinsky, Harold E. 1972. *Police Decisions to Report Offenses*. Philadelphia: University of Pennsylvania (dissertation).

Quinney, Richard. 1970. *The Social Reality of Crime*. Boston: Little, Brown and Company.

Quinney, Richard. 1974. *Critique of Legal Order: Crime Control in a Capitalist Society*. Boston: Little, Brown and Company.

Robison, Sophia M. 1936. *Can Delinquency be Measured?* New York: Columbia University Press.

Schur, Edwin M. 1968. *Our Criminal Society: Social and Legal Sources of Crime in America*. Englewood Cliffs, New Jersey: Prentice-Hall, Inc.

Smith, Richard Austin. 1961. 'The incredible electrical conspiracy'. *Fortune*, 63 (7 April):132–180 and (May):161–224.

Sudnow, David. 1965. 'Normal crimes: sociological features of the penal code in a public defender office'. *Social Problems*, 12 (Winter):255–276.

Sutherland, Edwin H. 1940. 'White-collar criminality'. *American Sociological Review*, 5 (February):1–12.

Sutherland, Edwin H. 1945. 'Is "white-collar crime" crime?' *American Sociological Review*, 10 (April):132–139.

Sutherland, Edwin H. 1961. *White-collar crime*. New York: Holt, Rinehart and Winston.

Tacitus (A. J. Church and W. J. Broderick, trans.; Hugh Lloyd-Jones, ed.). 1964. *Tacitus: The Annals and the Histories*. New York: Washington Square Press.

Tappan, Paul W. 1947. 'Who is the criminal?' *American Sociological Review*, 12 (February):96–102.

Tocqueville, Alexis de. 1945. *Democracy in America*. New York: Vintage Books.

United States Code. 1958. *Sherman Act*. U.S.C., title 15, secs. 1, 2.

Van der Sprenkel, Sybille. 1962. *Legal Institutions in Manchu China*. London: Athlone Press.

Veblen, Thorstein. 1899. *Theory of the Leisure Class*. Clifton, New Jersey: Augustus M. Kelley.

# 3. CONSTRAINTS ON THE AMERICAN ADMINISTRATOR: PRINCIPLED DECISIONS INDICATE INJUSTICE

## Introduction

It is a truism that administrators should apply the criminal law in a 'just' way, or, to put it in other words, that administrators should 'do justice' in their application of provisions of the criminal law. It is the thesis of this chapter that, ironically, systematically and rationally made (logically goal-oriented) decisions to apply the criminal law to particular cases indicate that injustice is being done.

Support for this thesis first requires that a definition be provided for what constitutes a 'just' decision. A definition is implicit in the Fifth and Fourteenth Amendments to the United States Constitution. 'Due process' must be afforded persons against whom the criminal law is applied, and persons to whom the law is applied must receive 'equal protection' in the pattern of application (at least in state jurisdictions, if not in the federal jurisdiction).

'Due process' and 'equal protection' address two different levels of the process of deciding how to apply the criminal law, though admittedly there has been some confusion in American courts' interpretations of these requirements. 'Due process' is the guarantee that a person has a set of procedures open to him or her to have and to provide information pertinent to the prospective application of the law. For example, this might include the right to present evidence at a formal hearing, or the right to have the assistance of counsel in presenting that evidence. Sometimes, this same meaning is given to the mandate of 'equal protection', especially in the provision of legal counsel (see United States Supreme Court, 1963a, and 1963b). However, 'equal protection' has an additional meaning of particular significance for the purposes of this discussion. Given information about cases, 'equal protection' means that administrators will apply the law in such a way that 'like cases are treated alike and different cases are treated differently' (Hart, 1961:155). For instance, the Supreme Court (1940) has decided that it is a denial of equal protection to exclude blacks from juries, intentionally and systematically, on the premise that all-white juries will tend to apply the law differently to white and black defendants in like-fact situations.

As it happens, there is a sizeable body of literature on the question of whether and when American jurors apply the criminal law justly. The problems faced by jurors in doing justice provide a nice illustration of problems faced by criminal justice administrators generally. Jury decision-making in the American context is therefore discussed in some detail in this chapter.

*Formal Basis of the Argument*

There is one, and only one area of life into which all men are born equal, and also remain equal throughout their lives, independent of physical, pecuniary, intellectual, or moral achievements (or other attributes): the pure game of chance. (Aubert, 1959:20)

The law leaves any administrator with discretion not only for the reasons outlined in chapter 1, but also because of problems of deciding 'what really happened' in most cases. Is a complainant or a suspect telling the truth? Is an eyewitness's identification of a person correct? Is someone's memory accurate? What was a suspect or defendant's 'true' state of mind when an act was committed? There are generally no infallible ways of answering these questions.

This leaves the conscientious administrator in a dilemma. What fallible criteria are to be applied to evidence to decide whether there is 'probable' or 'reasonable cause' or 'a preponderance' of evidence to believe something happened, or whether something happened 'beyond a reasonable doubt'? Typically, the administrator has very limited information about any case. But if the administrator succumbs to the problem and makes capricious evaluations of evidence in cases, he or she is open to a charge of irresponsibility. Administrators are expected to make decisions based on fixed and consistent ('objective') principles.

45

If decisions on how to apply the criminal law are to be based on principles independent of evidence in each case itself as to whether an unlawful act has been committed, the consistent use of the principles will bias the chances of the law being applied in this way or that. For instance, if principle states that defendants protesting innocence who perspire a lot are not to be believed, tendency to perspiration biases a person's chances of having the law applied against him or her. Since police believe that people with prior records are more likely guilty than others when newly accused of crimes, the chances of arrest of people with prior records are biased against them. And so on for any other principle that might be employed.

On the other hand, the only way to establish equal treatment of persons under the law is to equalise the chances that any of these factors will weigh in anyone's favour. This brings us to Aubert's statement quoted at the outset of this section. Any explanation of principles that systematically account for application of the law implies that people who happen to fall into different categories in the social system, independently of the terms of the law, and independently of the content of evidence in each case, have different probabilities of the law being applied for or against them. Everyone would be treated alike before the law if administrators refused jurisdiction over all cases and did not apply the law to anyone. Failing that, the closest approximation that could be made to prospective like treatment of like cases (given unequal probabilities of cases coming before the administrators) would be for all administrators to make purely random decisions as to whether to apply a provision of the criminal law against anyone they were given to suspect of a violation of the law. Hence, demands that administrators of the law accept responsibility for making 'reasoned' and 'objective' judgements about evidence they receive amounts to a demand that they indicate the doing of injustice.

Nevertheless, the ethic of doing justice is strong enough in our criminal justice system to require some argument that systematic application of the law can be considered just. Aubert outlines this fallback position:

Election to a jury by lot may be viewed as a just way of distributing inevitable burdens (of administration). But it is also perceived as one means by which independence and objectivity of the courts are secured. The juror, like the lay judge (in Norway), is the representative of the people in an activity which is largely professional and therefore hard to control. Since he is untrained, he performs his role under some suspicion of emotionalism and partiality. The election by lot secures, however, a minimum of independence. Nobody can designate him with a view to his subjective disposition *vis-à-vis* one or the other of the contending parties. That decision is left to chance. Although this gives no guarantee that the juror will be an unbiased person, it does prevent the occurrence of systematic biases in any particular case, both in fact and in appearance. (Aubert, 1959:17)

Clarifying what prevention of systematic biases means, Aubert further states:

What is then achieved is not that each contribution or merit receives its just reward, but that it can be established that rewards and punishments are at least unrelated to those criteria that are deemed as irrelevant biases. (Aubert, 1959:20–21)

This is to say that if it is difficult to account for the effects on case outcomes of biases that the administrator uses in making decisions, the administrator will be protected from criticism for exercise of his or her prejudices. There is good reason to accept the premise that any administrator is bound to apply the law with a bias or biases, to be sure. However, to sustain a general faith in the justice of administrators' actions, the courts and social scientists have tended to turn this premise on its head. The premise typically used in evaluations of administrators' actions becomes: an administrator is presumed to be doing justice unless the particular bias that affects an application of the law can be empirically isolated and described.

Evidence to overcome the latter premise may be of two kinds. The evidence can either be that which describes the kind of person apt to be put in the position of administrator (here termed 'circumstantial evidence' of bias in application of the law), or that which describes what kind of application of the law (favouring one class of persons over another) is more likely to be made than another (here termed 'direct evidence' of bias in application of the law). In the case of jurors as administrators, this means that bias is adequately shown by convincing evidence that one kind of person is more likely than another to be chosen as a juror, or that those chosen as jurors are apt to give competent evidence in one form a greater weight than that in another form, in a way not covered by law.

In the survey of literature of jury decision-making that follows, the reader is likely to detect a 'Catch-22' or double bind that faces the administrator who is called upon to do justice. The things for which American administration of the law is impeached are the very things that are also demanded of administration in the name of 'due process'. In the name of due process, those affected by the administration of the law are supposed to have sufficient information (a) to assess the competency of administrators to apply the law, and (b) to account for the way in which administrators will weigh evidence in matters before them. This is the same kind of information that tends to establish which class or classes of persons will be favoured by the law's application. If administrators tend to give indication of injustice, so do those who investigate their efforts, sometimes with the kind of vengeance revealed in this quotation:

> Our study is only a beginning. The numbers involved were too small to be statistically significant. Our questions were perhaps not perfect. But inconclusive as our results are, they do indicate that there are some deficiencies in the jury system, and that the magnitude of those deficiencies is measurable. Let us hope that future investigators will continue to perform the detailed and time consuming work necessary to give dependable results. (Hoffman and Brodley, 1952:250)

The measured success of such research efforts is the credibility of their demonstration that administrators bring particular biases to bear in their applications of the law.

On the one hand, maintenance of the myth of administrators' doing justice requires that their applications of the law remain unpredictable and unexplained. On the other hand, adequate social response to administrative decisions requires that those decisions become predictable and explained. The structure of the American criminal law system puts the credibility of the *justice* of application of the law on the one hand and of *knowledge* about application of the law on the other into irreconcilable conflict.

*Use of Circumstantial Evidence*

The United States Supreme Court (1935) has established the rule that it will review evidence and reverse a state conviction based on proof that black citizens are 'intentionally and systematically' excluded from the grand jury that hands down the indictment, under the authority of the 'equal protection' clause of the Fourteenth Amendment. The Court (1946) has applied the same principle under authority of the United States Judicial Code in reversing the convictions of defendants in federal court by petit juries from which women were excluded. Apparently, unless it can be shown that the exclusion of a class of jurors is intentional as well as systematic, the Supreme Court is unwilling to pass judgment on whether the exclusion is substantial enough to be unlawful (see, e.g., United States Supreme Court, 1945). Otherwise, the Court is unwilling to move beyond the presumption that jurors are 'truly representative of the community' and therefore unbiased in their application of the law.

Finkelstein (1966) and Kariys (1972) have taken the position that it is unnecessary for the Court to go so far as to demand evidence of intentional exclusion of classes of jurors. If one class of persons is shown statistically to be more likely than another to be seated on juries in a given jurisdiction (at an arbitrary level of significance such as 0.05), these authors argue that this should constitute legally sufficient circumstantial evidence that juries are doing injustice.

The argument implies the availability of background information on jurors and the community from which they come. Emerson (1968) goes so far as to advocate that the background information should include personality test results for prospective jurors, not only for judicial determination that jurors are representative of the 'communities', but for use by attorneys in jury screening. This carries us back to the implicit rationale for judicial reluctance to adduce any but the strongest evidence of exclusion of certain classes of jurors. As Okun (1968) puts it, if 'scientific' data on prospective jurors became available to lawyers (and by extension to the courts on review), these administrators would be expected to use the information to introduce new biases into the application of the law. The ideal state of affairs, argues Okun, would be to make the selection of jurors 'truly random'.

Making selection of jurors 'truly random' would require three major changes in current American jury selection processes. First of all, if the juries were to represent all the 'peers' of any prospective defendant in a given jurisdiction, jury lists would have to include all residents of the jurisdiction who would be old enough and competent to be tried if charged in a court. Second, when the random selection of petit and grand jurors was made from the list, no person could be excluded (such as lawyers or those with felony records in many jurisdictions) or excused (such as women until recently in New York State) from jury service. Third, everyone randomly selected for jury service would have to be seated on juries in random sequence. Judges and attorneys could not have jurors excluded peremptorily or for cause. Over time and across cases in a jurisdiction, this is the only way to ensure that jurors are selected without bias to apply the law.

This leads to a dilemma that systems theorists refer to as 'crossing system levels'. Truly random selection of jurors is based on the theory that the biases of individual jurors will cancel one another. As Belli (1963:771) puts it, even in one case, the chance that a particular bias of an individual juror will be reflected in a vote of six or twelve or more petit or grand jurors is theoretically expected to be remote (e.g., perhaps one chance in 12! of a unanimous vote of twelve jurors). Critics of this position point to the possibility that one juror's bias can have a significant effect on application of the law in a particular case, and argue that where any prospective juror is shown to have a particular predisposition to apply the law in one way rather than another, that prospective juror should be excluded from hearing a case. This argument leads to a preference for systematic rather than random selection of jurors. Controlling for selection bias at the aggregate level necessarily permits selection bias at the individual level, and vice versa. The current combination of approaches to jury selection, in an attempt to rise above this dilemma, permits introduction of biases at both levels. Theoretically, there is no escape from the introduction of bias into any juror selection process. Theoretically, too, such bias can be expected circumstantially to affect jurors' decisions as to how to apply the law, and thereby to contribute to indicating that injustice is being done.

This leads back to Aubert's statement about how jury selection can increase the chances that the jury verdict will be viewed as just. As an effort is made to guard the secrecy of information about jury deliberations, so the optimal jury selection strategy would keep the availability of information about jurors, prospective, presently serving, or who have already served, to an absolute minimum. The only information available to court clerks, judges, attorneys and social scientists would be that sufficient to get a prospective juror to appear in court — i.e., the prospective juror's name and where he could be physically located. This would represent an attempt to keep the bias in juror selection unknown, so that those selecting jurors could not make systematic use of the bias and that those who reviewed the jury selection could not describe any particular bias and make it manifest. In this way, the aura of doing justice in jury selection might effectively be maintained.

Of course this strategy falls foul of the principles of due process and of rational social evaluation and change, and therefore cannot be expected to be implemented successfully. The body of knowledge about outcomes of jury selection processes and their relevance to jurors' applications of the law can be expected to grow steadily, and with this growth a continual confrontation that jury selection indicates the injustice of the application of the law, can be anticipated.

*Use of Direct Evidence*

Direct evidence correlates either characteristics of jurors or structural features of the trial with particular kinds of jury verdict. In an experimental setting, Boehm (1968) found that more youthful jurors and those with authoritarian attitudes returned guilty verdicts in cases they heard, while the older and more anti-authoritarian jurors were more likely to find guilt of a lesser offence than that charged and to vote for acquittal. Mitchell and Byrne (1973) also found experimentally that authoritarian jurors were more likely than others to vote for conviction when the defendant was cast as a socially acceptable target. In other experiments on the characteristics of jurors, Stephan (1973) found that jurors tended to be more lenient in votes on cases involving same-sex defendants (leading her to the conclusion that women defendants are discriminated against, given the low representation nationwide of women on juries), while Becker *et al.* (1965) found that Catholic jurors were more likely than others to vote conviction in a euthanasia case.

Some results of survey or field research supplement these experimental data. Reed (1965) found that jurors in Louisiana were more likely to convict defendants if the jurors had no prior jury service, if they were natives of South Louisiana (as against North Louisiana and the rest of the United States), and at the higher levels of occupation and education of jurors. Robinson (1950) found that federal jurors with pro-labour attitudes were the more likely grand jurors to indict members of management in cases of labour disputes.

Note well: these data inform us as to how biases in jury decision-making may be discovered, but the data do not point the way to eliminating biases. Some patterns of bias are apt to be differentially associated with applications of the law by authoritarian, male, young, Catholic, pro-labour and/or first-service jurors, perhaps from a given geographical area, other patterns with applications of the law by anti-authoritarian, female, old, non-Catholic, anti-labour and/or veteran jurors, perhaps from other areas. Other patterns of bias can be expected to be associated with applications of the law by various combinations of types of jurors. It can be expected that biases in jury decision-making can be *varied* by selection of specific types of jurors, but *not* that biases *per se* can be *eliminated*. The *appearance* of just applications of the law can only be maintained in the absence of knowledge of what the biases may be. Inversely, studies in which biases are inferred serve merely to indicate the doing of injustice; they cannot facilitate maintenance of the appearance of doing justice.

There is another kind of direct evidence of bias in jury decision-making. This is evidence of the effect of the way information is presented to jurors at trial. Broeder (1965) found in interviews of jurors that knowledge of the occupations of defendants affected the votes of the jurors. Tans and Chaffee (1966) found experimentally that pre-trial information (or publicity) about a case reinforced pro-prosecution biases of jurors. Stone (1969) found experimentally that asking jurors for a tentative decision on application of the law after the presentation of some evidence tended to affect the jurors' final verdicts, by which he held that findings of 'primary effects' on jury decision-making could be explained. By implication, one could change jury verdicts by eliminating information about the occupations of defendants, by eliminating pre-trial information altogether, and/or by encouraging jurors to refrain from judging a case until all available information had been received, reversing the effects of existing sources of bias. Here too, data on biasing influences on jury decision-making can be employed to alter biases, but not to eliminate bias *per se*. In the final analysis, information as to sources of juror bias can be used to select biases, but in this form of social engineering injustice will appear where once it was assumed that justice was being done.


## Conclusion:
## American Administrators' Strategy

The phenomenon of indicating injustice applies equally to all administration of the criminal law. Jurors are only a case in point. Fundamentally, indicating injustice in any administration of the criminal law is accomplished simply by accounting for how decisions as to application of the law are made. By definition, both theoretically and operationally, a bias in application of the law is an account of a basis for the choice of application. The bias can be founded on ethical principle, but it remains a bias and the resultant application of the law is therefore by definition unjust.

This leaves social planners and other administrators in an inescapable dilemma. In so far as they choose to account for the way in which decisions are or should be made to apply the criminal law, they manifestly support the existence of biases in the decision-making. In so far as they choose to support the appearance of justice in decision-making, they manifestly support ignorance of the way in which decisions are or should be made.

Generally speaking, administrators of the criminal law appear at least implicitly to understand this dilemma. There are some fairly clear parameters to the typical strategy employed by administrators to cope with the dilemma. The strategy is directed to conveying the impression that administration represents a 'government of law' and not 'of men' (see, e.g., Kalven and Zeisel, 1966:8).

The strategy has six major elements. One element is the claim that the administrator exercises individual judgement peculiar to him or her in applying the law, and that one can understand the operation of the exercise of judgement with the 'expertise' of one who has directly, personally experienced having to make the application of the law to particular cases. Another element is resistance to close scrutiny of the way in which administrative decisions are made, on the grounds that such scrutiny interferes with or otherwise biases the ability of the administrator to obtain and/or process information. In concert, these two elements retard the accountability of administrative decision-making, thus supporting the maintenance of the appearance (or the possibility) that justice is being done.

The third and fourth elements together are a bow to the demand for accountability. The first of these elements is an effort to have operational criteria for official evaluation of any administrator made explicit by someone other than the administrator himself or herself. The judge's instructions to the jury and the use of numbers of felony arrests as a measure of the police officer's performance are examples of making such criteria explicit. The second of these elements is what Blau (1955) and others have called 'goal displacement'. Ostensibly, the meeting of the operational criteria for official evaluation is a means to higher ends in the application of the criminal law. However, for the administrator, conforming to these criteria is apt to become an end in itself. This permits the administrator to claim that his or her application of the law is principled, while abdicating personal responsibility for choice of the bias inherent in the principle. The administrator can hope that his or her critics will be forced into reasoning that if something other than the administrator himself or herself dictates a bias on which to base application of the law, the administrator personally makes the decision 'under law', not 'under men'. Indeed, the reasoning is incorporated into the English and American common law in at least one form, as the principle of *stare decisis* or 'rule of precedent'. If a decision is made 'under law', the decision may conclusively be presumed to be just, such that with reference to a presumably superhuman referent, the law itself, like cases are treated alike.

The typical American administrator's hope for appearing to be a mere servant of the law may be fulfilled, in practice at least, on a short-term basis. The reasoning has the status in our society of a cliché, and critics who challenge the reasoning are open to the charge of disregarding 'common sense'. However, when the argument is made (as in chapter 2) that a socio-economic bias inheres in the terms of the law themselves, the reasoning collapses. Administrators increase this liability to charges of doing injustice by any demonstration of adherence to principle in their decision-making. The fifth element of administrative strategy is an attempt to counter this liability. Administrators are apt to lobby for revision and extension of the law they apply, to generate new areas of discretion and stay ahead of knowledge of the principles of their application of the law, and to keep at least

54

some areas of decision-making safe from discovery of bias.

The sixth element, on the other hand, is an attempt to neutralise criticism from the clients with whom the criminal justice system deals directly. The typical administrator will be moved in rational self-interest to aim to apply the law so as to favour the appropriative interests of those perceived to be the more socially powerful among those he or she faces. Administration of the law is at least in part a matter of building political alliances.

This strategy is what one would be led to expect of American administrators from the constraints imposed on them by the structure of the law. It remains to be seen whether administrators do as they might.

REFERENCES

Aubert, Vilhelm. 1959. 'The role of chance in social affairs'. *Inquiry*, 2 (Spring):1—24.
Becker, Theodore L., Donald C. Hildum and Keith Bateman. 1965. 'The influence of jurors' values on their verdicts: a courts and politics experiment'. *Southwestern Social Science Quarterly*, 46 (September): 130—140.
Belli, Melvin M. 1963. *Modern Trials*. Indianapolis: Bobbs-Merrill Co.
Blau, Peter M. 1955. *The Dynamics of Bureaucracy*. Chicago: University of Chicago Press.
Boehm, Virginia R. 1968. 'Mr. Prejudice, Miss Sympathy, and the authoritarian personality: an application of psychological measuring techniques to the problem of jury bias'. *Wisconsin Law Review*, 1968 (no. 3):734—747.
Broeder, Dale W. 1965. 'Occupational expertise and bias as affecting juror behavior: a preliminary look'. *New York University Law Review*, 40 (December):1029—1100.
Emerson, C. David. 1968. 'Personality tests for prospective jurors'. *Kentucky Law Journal*, 56 (Summer):832—854.
Finkelstein, Michael O. 1966. 'The application of statistical decision theory to the jury discrimination cases'. *Harvard Law Review*, 80 (December):338—376.
Hart, H. L. A. 1961. *The Concept of Law*. Oxford: Clarendon Press.
Hoffman, Harold M., and Joseph Brodley. 1952. 'Jurors on trial'. *Missouri Law Review*, 17 (June):235—251.
Kalven, Harry Jr., and Hans Zeisel. 1966. *The American Jury*. Boston: Little, Brown and Company.
Kariys, David. 1972. 'Juror selection: the law, a mathematical method of analysis, and a case study'. *American Criminal Law Review*, 10 (Summer):771—806.
Mitchell, Herman E., and Donn Byrne. 1973. 'The defendant's dilemma: effects of jurors' attitudes and authoritarianism on judicial decisions'. *Journal of Personality and Social Psychology*, 25 (January):123—129.
Okun, Joshua. 1968. 'Investigation of jurors by counsel: its impact on the

decisional process'. *Georgetown Law Journal*, 56 (May): 839–879.

Reed, John P. 1965. 'Jury deliberations, voting, and verdict trends'. *Southwestern Social Science Quarterly* (March):361–370.

Robinson, W. S. 1950. 'Bias, probability and trial by jury'. *American Sociological Review*, 15 (February):73–78.

Stephan, Cookie. 1973. 'Sex prejudice in jury simulation'. (Paper presented at 68th Annual Meeting of the American Sociological Association, New York, 27 August.)

Stone, Vernon A. 1969. 'A primacy effect in decision-making by jurors'. *Journal of Communication*, 19 (September):239–247.

Tans, Mary Dee, and Steven H. Chaffee. 1966. 'Pretrial publicity and juror prejudice'. *Journalism Quarterly*, 43 (Winter):647–654.

United States Supreme Court.

    1935. *Norris v. Alabama*. 294 U.S. 587.

    1940. *Smith v. Texas*. 311 U.S. 398.

    1945. *Akins v. Texas*. 325 U.S. 398.

    1946. *Ballard et al. v. United States*. 329 U.S. 173.

    1963a. *Douglas v. California*. 372 U.S. 353.

    1963b. *Gideon v. Wainright*. 372 U.S. 335.

## 4. AMERICAN POLICE DECISION-MAKING[1]

*Introduction*

This chapter considers whether the theoretically indicated strategy for American administrators is followed in practice. The chapter is a case study of decision-making by American police. In the course of research (see Pepinsky, 1972) corroborated by reports to him by other researchers and members of police organisations, the present author has repeatedly been told by police personnel in various locales that police officers' applications of the law are based on expert, individual, independently unfathomable judgement. The first element of the strategy described at the end of chapter 3 is thus applied more often than not by police personnel. In the course of the same experience, the author has witnessed the commonness (though admittedly not the universality) of resistance of all levels of members of police organisations to observation and study of decision-making in those organisations. There is also an ethic among American police of keeping each other's misdeeds secret (Westley, 1970). Thus, the police usually employ the second element of the strategy. Customarily, police organisations actively take positions in favour of many proposed legislative changes, such as those concerning gun control and drug usage and marketing, adopting the fifth element of the hypothetical strategy.

Police conformity in practice to these three elements of the strategy, which are indicated for American administrators in the theory, is rather apparent. Whether police look to others for criteria to evaluate their performance, whether they displace goals of performance, and whether they tend to favour the socially powerful in their decisions: these matters of day-to-day decision-making are harder to infer, and have been the subject of much research.

57

One of the external authorities that American police rely on to provide principles for applying the law is a tradition inherited from predecessors as to what constitutes good police work. Niederhoffer (1967) has described a process by which new police officers learn the tradition from their seniors. In part, the tradition consists of certain stereotypes about which features of a situation signal occasions for law-enforcement activity. As the stereotypes become learned and internalised, the police have been found to use them as a basis for deciding whether an allegation of harm to which they are called to react should be treated as an offence. In turn, conformity by citizens to these stereotypes of offence behaviour is reinforced and fulfils what Merton (1957:475—490) calls 'a self-fulfilling prophecy'.

One of the most interesting and best-documented of these stereotypes is the belief that when a black assaults another black (particularly with a knife), the conflict will turn out to have been an ordinary family quarrel, whereas when both parties are white, the matter will be regarded as highly unusual and serious (LaFave, 1962, cited in Skolnick, 1966:171). While Black's (1970:744—746) data do not show support for the role of race in offence-reporting, his findings might have been different had he analysed harms involving the person separately from those involving only property. A basis for the stereotype that some groups 'ordinarily' do more serious violence to one another than do others has been provided by the work of Wolfgang and Ferracuti (1967). There is good reason to believe that patrolmen reinforce the tendency of citizens to act out the stereotype by treating violent offences among minority group members as commonplace and tolerable and among whites as exceptional and intolerable.

Uniformed patrolmen assigned the responsibility of traffic enforcement are commonly asked to find drivers who are not driving under proper authorisation from the state. This includes drivers who are driving under suspended or revoked licences, those driving without proper car registration, and, in some jurisdictions, those driving without proof of insurance. The patrolmen may also be asked to locate drivers with warrants outstanding against them for failure to pay traffic fines, as was the case in Minneapolis.

Under these circumstances, the patrolmen need criteria for stopping some drivers who have not just been seen violating the law. For this purpose, patrolmen in Minneapolis (Pepinsky, 1972) were found to rely on another self-fulfilling prophecy related to race. The prophecy is that minority group members driving relatively dilapidated cars are those most likely to be unauthorised to drive or to have outstanding warrants. It may be, for instance, that white drivers of expensive new cars are as likely to be driving under suspended licences as their counterparts, but this hypothesis remains untested. Since violators are found only among the group stopped by the police, the patrolmen can honestly say that the data 'show' that minority group drivers of dilapidated cars are those most likely to be driving under arrest warrants or without proper authorisation.

The Minneapolis study (Pepinsky, 1972) also provided a small number of cases which suggest that other stereotypes are operative in patrolmen's reactive decision-making. Where the complainant knows an alleged suspect, the patrolmen believe that he can settle such matters as thefts informally. Elderly complainants can safely be regarded as senile. Their complaints tend to be ignored. Women are to be protected, and the patrolmen treat their complaints of assault more seriously than those of males.

## Meeting Others' Demands

There are other cues the patrolmen get to indicate that treatment of a situation warrants formal law-enforcement activity, in the form of demonstrations of which response is socially expected of them. As several authors (including Bittner, 1967a; Bittner, 1967b; Cumming et al., 1965; Stoddard, 1967; and Wilson, 1963) have suggested, the policemen look for instruction from others as to whether they are presented with a situation that calls for formal law-enforcement action — as by an offence report or an arrest. The first clue the patrolmen receive as to what is expected of them is in the dispatcher's call. The present author (Pepinsky, 1972) found in fact that patrolmen whom he observed based their decisions on whether to report most offences practically entirely on whether the dispatcher mentioned an offence in his call, provided only that the patrolmen talked to someone who corroborated the call. This is consistent with Skolnick's (1966) and James Q. Wilson's (1968) observations that police feel impelled to demonstrate to those in a position to hear that they give priority to law-enforcement activity.

The expectation most commonly referred to in the literature is the explicit request or demand by a complainant that the police take specified action. Black (1970) found that police rely on complainants' expressed wishes to decide whether to report offences. Black and Reiss (1970) and Hohenstein (1969) report the same reliance on complainants' wishes in police decisions as to whether to take juveniles into custody.

Pollak (1950) has argued that a great deal of hidden female criminality exists, which he attributes in large measure to females' being treated as offenders by police much less readily than men. Here again a self-fulfilling prophecy apparently operates. Given the stereotype that women commit fewer crimes than men, patrolmen less often reactively treat women as offenders than they do men, and thus fewer women than men turn out to be offenders in official eyes.

Though hard data on the point are unavailable, officers in narcotics, morals and organised crime units apparently base their decisions to enter into law-enforcement activity on self-fulfilling prophecies initiated by citizen informants. The officers receive information as to identities, locations, and alleged conduct of suspects from the informants. The informants may be motivated to provide intelligence for personal power, material gain, lenience from the police, revenge, or, in rare instances, moral indignation.

Once the suspect is identified, if his or her alleged conduct meets departmental expectations as to conduct worthy of police attention, it is practically foreordained that the officers of the specialised unit will do their best to gather evidence for his or her arrest and prosecution. Bribery or further intelligence from the suspect may alter this course of action, but there are insufficient data to analyse decision-making in these contingencies.

Otherwise, rumour has it that there is but one other exception to this pattern of police activity. In some areas, morals squad officers are said to work out 'understandings' with known prostitutes. Periodically, at the convenience of the prostitute, she will submit to arrest and plead guilty to a minor charge provided she is left free to ply her trade in the meantime. In this way, the morals squad officer meets a more or less formal quota of arrests of prostitutes with the prostitutes' full cooperation. This exception to the use of the self-fulfilling prophecy criterion by narcotics, morals, and organised crime officers appears to be isolated, however.

The research by Terry (1967) suggests the operation of another self-fulfilling prophecy in the reactive decisions of 'juvenile officers' (an American term for officers who deal with juvenile cases) to treat problem cases as officially recognised instances of delinquency. A prior record of juvenile delinquency indicates that a case should be formally disposed of, thereby increasing the relative proportion of those regarded as delinquent that consists of juveniles seen who are 'known recidivists'. The criterion used by juvenile officers for their decisions becomes the basis for the rationale that more delinquents, 'after all' (see Garfinkel, 1956), have that characteristic.

One way of posing the question of whether legitimate and respectable control has been accomplished is to ask whether control through treatment of cases as demanding law enforcement is needed. Stereotypes are learned by policemen in the course of their careers. As Rubinstein (1973:150–151) notes, the stereotypes become clearer to policemen as their experience increases. Together, the stereotypes constitute 'street wisdom'. Certain categories of people clearly need to be treated as offenders. Why? Because they have tended to be those found likely to be offenders in the past. The reasoning is circular but powerful to the policeman who has no independent way of testing the power or of knowing the origin of the stereotypes.

Black (1970) found that patrolmen were more likely to file official reports in cases they believed they could present as felonies rather than as mere misdemeanours. Rubinstein (1973) reports misdemeanours resulting in arrest more often than violations. Since the patrolman knows that official action against more serious offences connotes more effective enforcement to his superiors, he (or now occasionally she) shapes his (or her) decisions to this expectation.

The reactive decisions of detectives fall overwhelmingly into the category of meeting expectations. The detectives react to offence reports, most of them received from patrolmen. Year by year, the Federal Bureau of Investigation (annual) reports that nationally detectives 'unfound' only 4 per cent of the reports they receive (i.e. decide that no offence has in fact occurred). The only meaningful prediction to be made about detectives' reactive decisions as to whether to treat cases as involving violations of the law is that every case will be so treated. Detectives apparently see it as their duty to treat all cases

61

they receive as involving offences, and they practically always meet this expectation.

Most stops of cars for traffic violations are a matter of meeting expectations. Quite simply, unless a patrolman is on the way to an emergency call (see Rubinstein, 1973:93), he is typically expected by superiors to stop anyone seen to commit a moving violation.

There are a couple of exceptions to this rule. First, if the violating driver will be too hard to catch, he is to be left alone. For example, if a car is going in the opposite direction to a patrolman on a heavily travelled street at high speed, the danger of a high-speed chase with little chance of catching the offending driver is apt to lead to a decision not to pursue.

Second, there are some established conventions in various departments about tolerable violations of traffic laws. It is unusual to stop a driver for exceeding the speed limit by a mere five miles per hour. In some areas, rolling slowly through a stop sign at a quiet intersection will be tolerated. Thus, uniformed policemen are usually expected by superiors to stop traffic violators unless (a) their presence is immediately required elsewhere, (b) catching the offending driver is impracticable, or (c) the traffic offence is within tolerable limits. Non-uniformed officers seldom make traffic stops at all.

Patrolmen generally abhor writing parking tickets. They will do so only if a strong demand is made, as by (a) a sergeant (see Rubinstein, 1973:46), (b) a private citizen under personal duress (e.g., whose driveway is blocked, see Rubinstein, 1973:157), or (c) by the owner of a commercial establishment (see Rubinstein, 1973:156).

Meeting expectations and fulfilling prophecies represent adoption of the third element of the strategy of maintaining the appearance of doing justice — taking the operational criteria for evaluation of one's work from someone else in a position of authority. The police attempt to absolve themselves of personal responsibility for application of the law by having the application rest on other's decisions.

Meeting expectations and fulfilling prophecies are also instances of goal displacement. Meeting others' standards becomes an end in itself, displacing personal responsibility for figuring out how to make just decisions. Doing as others ask and adherence to prior law-enforcement practice become stubborn defences against charges of unjust law enforcement. Mastery of such standard law-enforcement practice comes to be part of what the police call 'street wisdom', which the present author was told in Minneapolis takes five years to acquire, and which represents a substantial part of police claims to esoteric expertise.

*Responses to Demeanour*

It has repeatedly been found that those juvenile suspects whose demeanour toward the police is cooperative (see Black and Reiss, 1970; Chambliss and Nagasawa, 1969; and Piliavin and Briar, 1964) earn more lenience from the police than do those whose demeanour shows a lack of respect (see Goldman, 1963; LaFave, 1962; and LaFave, 1965). Black (1970) found that the more cooperative complainants were with the police, the more likely the police were to report offences. Reiss (1971:51) found that patrolmen were more hostile or authoritarian and more likely to ridicule citizens of both races when 'the citizens were agitated' than when they were 'calm and detached'. Though not all directly on point, this literature lends considerable support to regarding citizen demeanour as a major criterion of reactive decisions by patrolmen and juvenile officers as to whether to treat situations as instances of violation of law. One New York City Police captain who has given training to patrolmen on the handling of domestic disputes confirms that, in the case of alleged family 'assaults' at least, patrolmen generally arrest only when they receive abuse, regardless of threat or injury to other citizens.

There are findings (e.g. by Thornberry, 1973, in police decisions relating to juveniles, though not supported by such findings as those of Terry, 1967) that police in situations other than those involving intra-racial violence among private persons are more apt to treat cases involving minority group suspects as warranting formal law enforcement than cases involving whites. In part, this is attributable to the demeanour of police and of private persons toward one another. Bayley and Mendelsohn (1968:122—137) found in Denver that more minority group members reportedly experienced mistreatment by the police and complained about police than did whites. Biderman *et al.* (1967:137) found, in Washington, DC, that whites are consistently and generally substantially more 'pro-police' than blacks. It is therefore to be expected that minority group citizens are more likely to be antagonistic toward the police than are whites, as indeed the present author observed in Minneapolis.

Demeanour plays an important role in traffic law enforcement, too. Once a stop has taken place, demeanour is used as a criterion of whether the policeman will 'write a tag'. This motivation is exemplified by the police handling of some traffic matters. From informal observation in the Minneapolis study (Pepinsky, 1972:47—49), this is what happened during a typical encounter between a patrolman and a motorist he had approached. They talked for about a minute and then the officer waved at the motorist and returned to the squad car. He seemed a little nonplussed as he reported to his partner, 'I asked the guy if he knew what he'd done and he told me, "Yes sir, I ran the red light". He was so honest I couldn't bring myself to write him a tag.' To the present author he added, 'I'll go out of my way for someone who tells me the truth, but if there's one thing I can't stand it's a guy who lies to me.' This appears to have been a common attitude among the policemen observed. It is corroborated by Rubinstein's observations of police in Philadelphia (1973:159). As a rule, then, traffic enforcement as the product of meeting expectations turns out to be used primarily to teach apparently recalcitrant drivers a lesson in respect for the law. Perhaps this would not be the case where ticket quotas or bribery are the practice, but at present these practices seem to be limited to isolated areas.

A chain of reasoning leads to a connection between accomplishment of legitimate and respectable control on the one hand, and the demeanour of citizens toward the police on the other. The police commonly hold the plausible assumption that citizens who respect the authority of the law are more likely to behave in adherence to the dictates of the law. In the typical view of the policeman, he does not act as an individual, but as an agent sworn to uphold the majesty of the law before the public. If a citizen behaves disrespectfully toward the officer, the citizen is not seen by the officer as merely showing disregard for the officer as an individual. The citizen is seen as disregarding the larger authority the officer believes he represents. Thus, disrespect to the officer represents evidence the officer is apt to think of as disrespect for the law itself — hence, of a citizen's determination not to adhere to the dictates of the law in the future.

In a few moments of contact, there is little an officer can do for long-term effect on a citizen's disposition to obey the law. Minimally, the officer can reward any manifestation of respect for him and punish any manifestation of disrespect, as elementary learning theory would appear to dictate. To take a complainant seriously and thus to reward him is to treat his complaint as deserving of law-enforcement activity, and vice versa. To punish a suspect is to invoke the weight of the criminal justice system against him as by arrest, and vice versa. Hence, in reactive decision-making by the police, citizen demeanour toward them is a rational criterion for choice of action most likely to accomplish legitimate and respectable law-enforcement control. Kirkham (1974:19), a criminologist who became a policeman better to learn whereof he taught, put it this way:

> Whatever the risk to himself every police officer understands that his ability to back up the lawful authority which he represents is the only thing which stands between civilization and the jungle of lawlessness.

Based on this goal-displacing premise, it becomes just for the policeman to respond adversely to those who challenge his authority and favourably to those who acknowledge it. The police tend to come to regard the enforcement of deference to themselves as an end in itself, with the law-enforcement rationale considered only in response to charges of injustice.

*Status Identification*

The principle of the use of status identification as a criterion for decision-making is divisible into two parts. If the decision-maker perceives the status of a subject of his decision to be desirable, the decision-maker will act to carry out the subject's wishes as the decision-maker perceives them. If the decision-maker perceives the status of a subject to be undesirable, the decision will be to act against the perceived wishes of the subject.

Status identification does not appear to be an important factor in reactive police decisions concerning possible offences against the person (like assault and murder). As noted above, these decisions seem to be a function of the combined effects of reliance on self-fulfilling prophecies

65

and citizen demeanour. Nevertheless, status identification appears to operate as a principle of decision-making in matters involving possible property offences and juvenile status offences (i.e. like truancy, behaviour not proscribed for adults). Nearly forty years ago, Robison (1936:27—29) observed that a disproportionate share of delinquents turned out to be from poverty backgrounds because the police were more apt to ascribe wrongdoing to those from 'the wrong side of the tracks'. Shortly thereafter, Johnson (1941) made similar observations about police treatment of adults, as in arrest decisions. Police discrimination against minority groups or low socio-economic status persons in reactive police decisions has since been corroborated in a number of studies, including those by Black (1970), Bordua (1960), Cochran (1971), Goldman (1963), Kephart (1957), Skolnick (1966), and Thornberry (1973).

Some have discounted the role of racial or socio-economic status discrimination in law enforcement. Green has taken this position, finding no racial discrimination in police arrest decisions concerning adults. He attributes the appearance of racial discrimination to 'the wider distribution among Negroes of lower social class characteristics associated with crimes' (1970:488). The close relationship between race and socio-economic status in the United States makes this distinction tenuous at best.

Terry (1967) found from time series data that severity and number of prior offences rather than race explained juvenile officers' decisions as to disposition of cases, though Thornberry (1973) found an independent effect of race or socio-economic status on such decisions using cohort data. Terry's findings cannot stand in any event, provided race and socio-economic status determine initial police decisions as to whether to record offences and as to how severe the recorded offences are to be.

Race as associated with socio-economic status thus appears to be a substantial factor in police decision-making. The higher the socio-economic status of a potential suspect, the greater the probability that police at any stage of reactive decision-making will opt out of treating cases as appropriate for formal law-enforcement activity. Where the racial or status identity of a potential suspect is unknown, Black's (1970) findings suggest that higher socio-economic status complainants have the higher probability of getting the police to opt for formal law-enforcement activity.

66

Status identification is a variant of Goffman's (1963) concept of 'role distance'. By setting himself in the position of adversary to those he perceives to be of low socio-economic status, the policeman hopes not to be identified as 'one of them'. The present author (Pepinsky, 1970) has suggested that the police aspire to achieving such status distance by eliciting confessions from suspects. Conversely, if the policeman follows the perceived wishes of a private person, he can hope to share an identity with the person that includes the status ascribed to that person. Thus, the policeman has an interest in cooperating with those citizens who appear to have a status which the policeman is satisfied with having ascribed to himself, as Black (1970) has found.

In one sense, control for the policeman means working for or against those he meets. The policeman's action gains respectability from its conformity to the expectations of respectable citizens as opposed to those of the unrespectable. The action is given legitimacy by the tautology found and described by Quinney (1970). The legal order tends to express the interests of the dominant stratum (or strata) of the society. This dominant group also consists of people at the top of the socio-economic hierarchy. Therefore, what those at the top of the order want is by definition officially legitimate, in contrast to what is desired by those at the bottom of the hierarchy.

Use of status identification meets the demands of the sixth element of the strategy of maintaining the appearance of doing justice, for lower social status is apt to correspond to lesser social power. Not only does status identification conceivably serve the purpose of enhancing the policeman's status; it also implies that those against whom the law is applied have the lesser capacity to challenge the application of the law as being unjust.

*Conclusion*

Descriptions of American police behaviour appear to be entirely consistent with the theoretical strategy logically indicated for enabling American administrators to minimise criticism of the injustice of their work, given the constraints imposed by the structure of the criminal law. It would be a bore to pile case study upon case study, and the reader can take it for granted that American administrators other than the police tend to follow much the same strategy. Research on court practice, for example, corroborates the point (e.g. the study by Galanter, 1974). The police and other administrators in the United States apparently do try to keep their choice of principles by which to apply the criminal law safe from discovery by others for the sake of their own professional survival. In the process, they permit others the luxury of believing that perhaps justice under law is being done after all.

There is no need to lay the blame for this strategy on base or evil motives of the administrators. Given the constraints imposed by the structure of the law, there is little reason to expect that any imagined set of 'good' people would follow a different course with a similar legal structure and a similar mandate to apply the law. If the strategy American administrators follow is to change, it is the structure within which administrators work and not the faces of administrators that must be altered.

Nor will more detailed specification of the terms of how the law is to be applied change the strategy by itself. Such specification will only create more room for administrators to keep to the strategy that reveals itself to be best suited to their rational self-interest. In its present form, American criminal law practically demands that administrators favour the appropriative interests of the wealthy over those of the poor. The form of the law practically decrees that administrators try to hide the principles by which they make decisions, and that they abdicate personal responsibility for the following principles that are nevertheless uncovered. If private citizens in the United States tend to distrust their administrators (as many proclaim they do), they have the structure of their criminal law to thank for their plight.

It has long been proclaimed that the primary end of the criminal law is to accomplish social control. And so it does. However, if a people are to accept the perpetuation of life with a particular system of criminal law, it behoves them to ask not only *whether* it controls, but *how* it controls as well. Perhaps the constraints the law imposes on administrators are unintended by those involved in legislation. Intentions alone do not determine constraints. Perhaps the structure of American criminal law should be maintained as it is, but inherent in that decision is the proposition that administrative behaviour patterns should remain as they are.

The situation is the same with many of the behaviour patterns among the general populace in the United States. The relationship between these behaviour patterns and the structure of American criminal law remains to be explored.

## NOTES

1. Thanks are given for permission to use some material from the present author's chapter, 'Police decision-making', in Don M. Gottfredson (ed.), *Decisions in the Criminal Justice System: Reviews and Essays in Decision-Making*, Washington, D. C.: National Institute of Mental Health (Crime and Delinquency Issues: Monograph Series, in press, 1976).

## REFERENCES

Bayley, David H., and Harold Mendelsohn. 1968. *Minorities and the Police: Confrontation in America*. New York: Free Press.

Biderman, Albert D., Louise A. Johnson, Jennie McIntyre and Adrienne W. Weir. 1967. 'Incidence of crime victimization', in President's Commission on Law Enforcement and Criminal Justice, Field Surveys I: *Report on a Pilot Study in the District of Columbia on Victimization and Attitudes Toward Law Enforcement*, ch. 2, pp. 26—118. Washington, DC: US Government Printing Office.

Bittner, Egon. 1967a. 'Police discretion in emergency apprehension of mentally ill persons'. *Social Problems*, 14 (Winter):278—292.

Bittner, Egon. 1967b. 'The police on skid row: a study of peace keeping'. *American Sociological Review*, 32 (October):699—715.

Black, Donald J. 1970. 'Production of crime rates'. *American Sociological Review*, 35 (August):733—747.

Black, Donald J., and Albert J. Reiss Jr. 1970. 'Police control of juveniles'. *American Sociological Review*, 35 (February):63—77.

Bordua, David J. 1960. 'Sociological theories and their implications for juvenile delinquency'. *Report of Children's Bureau Conference*. Washington, DC: United States Department of Health, Education and Welfare, vol. 2.

Chambliss, William, and Richard H. Nagasawa. 1969. 'On the validity of official statistics: a comparison study of white, black and Japanese high school boys'. *Research in Crime and Delinquency*, 6 (January): 71—77.

Cochran, Peggy. 1971. 'A situational approach to the study of police—Negro relations'. *The Sociological Quarterly*, 12 (Spring):232—237.

Cumming, Elaine, Ian Cumming and Laura Edell. 1965. 'Policeman as philosopher, guide and friend'. *Social Problems*, 12 (Winter):276—286.

Federal Bureau of Investigation. Annual *Uniform Crime Reports*. Washington, DC: United States Government Printing Office.

Galanter, Marc. 1974. 'Why the "haves" come out ahead: speculations on the limits of legal change'. *Law and Society Review* (Autumn):95—160.

Garfinkel, Harold, 1956. 'Conditions of successful degradation ceremonies'.

*American Journal of Sociology*, 61 (March):420–424.

Goffman, Erving. 1963. *Encounters: Two Studies in the Sociology of Interaction.* Indianapolis: Bobbs-Merrill.

Goldman, Nathan. 1963. *The Differential Selection of Juvenile Offenders for Court Appearance.* New York: National Council on Crime and Delinquency.

Green, Edward. 1970. 'Race, social status, and criminal arrest'. *American Sociological Review*, 35 (June):476–490.

Hohenstein, William F. 1969. 'Factors influencing the police disposition of juvenile offenders', in Thorsten Sellin and Marvin E. Wolfgang (eds), *Delinquency: Selected Studies*, pp. 138–149, New York: John Wiley and Sons.

Johnson, George B. 1941. 'The Negro and crime'. *The Annals of the American Academy of Political and Social Science*, 271 (September):93–104.

Kephart, William M. 1957. *Racial Factors and Urban Law Enforcement*, Philadelphia: University of Pennsylvania Press.

Kirkham, George L. 1974. 'A professor's street lessons'. *FBI Law Enforcement Bulletin*, 35 (March):14–22.

LaFave, Wayne R. 1962. 'The police and non-enforcement of the law'. *Wisconsin Law Review*, (no. 1) 5:104–137.

LaFave, Wayne R. 1965. *Arrest: The Decision to Take a Suspect into Custody.* Boston: Little, Brown and Company.

Merton, Robert K. 1957. *Social Theory and Social Structure.* New York: Free Press (rev. edn).

Niederhoffer, Arthur. 1967. *Behind the Shield: The Police in Urban Society.* Garden City, New York: Doubleday.

Pepinsky, Harold E. 1970. 'A theory of police reaction to Miranda v. Arizona'. *Crime and Delinquency*, 16 (October):379–392.

Pepinsky, Harold E. 1972. *Police Decisions to Report Offenses.* Philadelphia: University of Pennsylvania (dissertation).

Piliavin, Irving, and Scott Briar. 1964. 'Police encounters with juveniles'. *American Journal of Sociology*, 70 (September):206–214.

Pollak, Otto. 1950. *The Criminality of Women.* Philadelphia: University of Pennsylvania Press.

Quinney, Richard. 1970. *The Social Reality of Crime.* Boston: Little, Brown and Company.

Reiss, Albert J. 1971. *The Police and the Public.* New Haven: Yale University Press.

Robison, Sophia M. 1936. *Can Delinquency be Measured?* New York: Columbia University Press.

Rubinstein, Jonathan. 1973. *City Police.* New York: Farrar, Straus and Giroux.

Skolnick, Jerome H. 1966. *Justice Without Trial: Law Enforcement in a Democratic Society.* New York: John Wiley and Sons.

Stoddard, Ellwyn R. 1967. 'The informal code of police deviancy: a sociological approach to blue collar crime'. El Paso: University of Texas, unpublished paper.

Terry, Robert M. 1967. 'The screening of juvenile offenders'. *Journal of Criminal Law, Criminology and Police Science*, 58 (June):173–181.

Thornberry, Terence P. 1973. 'Race, socio-economic status and sentencing in the juvenile justice system'. *Journal of Criminal Law and Criminology*, 64 (March):90–98.

Westley, William A. 1970. *Violence and the Police: A Sociological Study of Law, Custom and Morality.* Cambridge, Mass.: Massachusetts Institute of Technology

Press.

Wilson, James Q. 1963. 'The police and their problems: a theory', in *Yearbook of the Graduate School of Public Administration*, pp. 8—13. Cambridge, Mass.: Harvard University Press.

Wilson, James Q. 1968. *Varieties of Police Behavior: the Management of Law and Order in Eight Communities*. Cambridge, Mass.: Harvard University Press.

Wolfgang, Marvin E., and Franco Ferracuti. 1967. *The Subculture of Violence: Towards an Integrated Theory in Criminology*. London: Tavistock Publications.

# PART II

# Response to the Criminal Law by the General Populace

## 5.  CONSTRAINTS ON THE GENERAL POPULACE: THE PRINCIPLE OF LEGALITY[1]

*Introduction*

The way in which the form of the law affects administrators could be seen rather directly. Manifestly, the law influences administrators and guides their work continuously in their daily routines. The effect of the form of the law on the daily routines of the American general populace is far harder to infer. Most people in American society are seldom, if ever, directly involved in the application of the criminal law. The connection between the criminal law and the daily routines among the populace is therefore apt to be indirect at best.

Nevertheless, there is good reason for believing that the connection between the form of the law and behaviour patterns among the general populace is substantial and significant. 'The crime problem' is a major topic of media concern and political debate in the United States. Americans are bombarded with television dramatisations of criminal justice operations (generally in idealised form). A range of ideas about what causes crime (e.g. broken families) and about what should be done in response to crime (e.g., 'lock 'em up and throw away the key') have practically become part of American folklore. These ideas have dominated American criminological thought for at least a century and a half with remarkably little change (as revealed by the work of Rothman, 1971). Even debate has tended to become stabilised around constant issues (e.g. that of whether offenders should be incapacitated, punished or rehabilitated). The experience of teaching introductory courses in criminology to American students reveals that most of the students already have highly developed cultural stereotypes about crime and criminal law. (Witness the written reaction of one beginning student who had just discovered that legal functionaries in criminal court typically assumed defendants were guilty: 'Surely this is not the American way!') It is fair to assume that those who learn to live in a culture develop some picture of what crime and criminal law are and should be and can be: a picture that is consistent with other culturally pervasive behaviour patterns that each resident experiences. Once developed, it is to be expected that the picture will be resistant to change, that the validity of the picture in one form will be relied upon for the sake of what some social psychologists (e.g. Rosenberg and Abelson, 1960) call 'cognitive consistency'. The other behaviour patterns that accompany the stereotype of crime and the criminal law would not necessarily be responsive to the structure of the law in the sense that the structure of the law comes first and then produces the other behaviour patterns. If the structure of the law reflects a stereotype and is consistent with values underlying other behaviour patterns, support for the stereotypic legal structure and for the other behaviour patterns are apt to be tied together by the force of consistency. So long as the structure of the law fits the stereotype, commitment to other behaviour should be reinforced by the force of consistency. Conversely, if the structure of the law were to change radically and noticeably to the general populace, pressure to change other behaviour patterns would be expected to be exerted for the sake of renewal of cognitive consistency. In addition, one would not expect sufficient popular support for radical change in the legal structure to occur unless commitment to other behaviour patterns became attenuated. As algae and fungus cause one another to survive symbiotically in the plant growth known as lichen, so the other behaviour by which a general populace responds to the structure of the criminal law can be explained as a symbiotic response to the form of the law.

How does one infer this symbiotic relationship? One method is to compare behaviour patterns in two polities, comparable in size and complexity, one polity having a highly developed system of formal written criminal law and the other having a small, rarely and inconstantly applied, body of written criminal law. If a basis in deductive logic can be found for associating differences in legal structure with major differences in other behaviour patterns, one can tentatively conclude (pending the discovery of disconfirming evidence) that one has discovered some rules by which popular response to a legal structure is governed.

Such a comparative approach is taken here. In order to begin to infer some popular behavioural responses to the structure of American criminal law, the structure of the law and behaviour patterns in the United States are contrasted with those in the People's Republic of China (PRC). To begin with, the logic that has led the Chinese to resist the development of formal written criminal law is reconstructed in this chapter. Popular behaviour patterns in the United States and in China are compared and related back to contrasting ideological perspectives on law in chapter 6.

## Development of Substantive Law in the PRC[2]

By 1949, China had a tradition of using criminal codes. The Ching or Manchu Dynasty (1644–1911) promulgated the Ta Ch'ing Lü-li with '436 sections that contain a greater number of statutes and approximately 1,800 sub-statutes' (Bodde and Morris, 1967:7). The Nationalist Government enacted a voluminous Code of the Six Laws. But the charter of government of the People's Republic of China (PRC), passed by the Communist Party Central Committee in 1949 and called the Common Programme, wiped away this heritage by stating simply at Article 17:

> All of the reactionary Kuomintang government's laws, decrees, and judicial systems shall be abolished. Laws and decrees that protect the people shall be adopted, and the people's judicial system shall be established.

The new criminal law enacted in the PRC was sparse. Article 7 of the Common Programme proscribed counter-revolutionary activity. This proscription was somewhat elaborated in 1951, in the Act of the PRC for the Punishment of Counter-Revolution (APCR). Its English translation is only three pages in length, and while its scope is broad, its detail is minimal. For example, our crimes of murder, manslaughter and assaults of all kinds are covered by a simple prohibition against 'attacking, killing or injuring people or public employees' (APCR art. 9(4)). Any of the acts, provided it is committed 'with a counter-revolutionary purpose', is punishable by death or life imprisonment unless 'the circumstances of their [the perpetrators'] cases are relatively minor', for which a minimum term of five years' imprisonment is prescribed (APCR, art. 9). Those found guilty of counter-revolutionary acts may also be deprived of their property and political rights (APC, art. 17). In contravention of the Western principle of legality, the law is made retroactive (APCR, art. 18).

Corruption was also prohibited by the Common Programme (art. 18), and in 1952 the Act of the PRC for Punishment of Corruption (APC) was promulgated. This law consisted of eighteen articles and defined corruption as 'all acts of embezzling, stealing, obtaining state property by fraud or by illegal speculation, extorting property of others by force, accepting bribes and other acts of unlawful profit-making that utilize public resources for private gain, by personnel of all state organs, enterprises, schools and their subordinate institutions' (APC, art. 2). What constitutes corruption is not further specified.

Cohen (1968: 315) summarises the substantive criminal law situation even as it now exists:

> The act for the punishment of counterrevolution and the act for punishment of corruption are the principal criminal laws promulgated by the PRC. There are also a few provisions of relatively narrow applicability, such as the Provisional Act for Punishment of Crimes that Endanger State Currency. In addition, numerous laws, such as the Marriage Law, simply state that their violation shall be punishable. [Citations omitted]

To meet a need for formalisation of a procedure to impose minor sanctions ('if the [wrongful] act does not warrant criminal sanctions', Security Administration Punishment Act of the PRC (SAPA), 1957: art. 2), one further law was later enacted. Fifteen days is the maximum jail sentence that can be imposed for violation of its provisions (SAPA, art. 3(3)). In some cases a fine of up to 30 yuan may be imposed (SAPA, art. 3(2)), contraband may be confiscated (SAPA, art. 3(4)) and restitution may be ordered (SAPA, art. 29). Relatively detailed lists of proscribed acts are contained in arts. 5—15 of the law, from gang fighting to intentionally damaging flowers, grass or trees in parks or on the sides of streets. SAPA, art. 31, provides that 'acts which violate security administration but which are not enumerated in this Act may, by comparison with the most similar clauses of Articles 5 to 15 of this act', also be punished subject to review. As Cohen (1968:220) observes, acts not enumerated in the Act have indeed been punished without hesitation.

Work was begun on a draft criminal code, but the draft was never made public and the effort abandoned with the advent of the Anti-Rightist Movement beginning in 1957. This movement and the SAPA mark the end of the development of formal substantive (and procedural) criminal law in the PRC. To the critics of the Hundred Flowers Period, a brief time during which attacks on the state and the Party were encouraged immediately preceding the Anti-Rightist Movement, it appeared that 'a state of confusion exists in the promulgation of laws and decrees and the issuance of directives by the State Council, its various offices and the various ministries' (New China News Agency, 27 May 1957, translated in MacFarquhar, 1960:210–211). Most offices charged with administering the laws were viewed as being 'without law to follow' (Kuang-ming Jih-pao, 1 June 1957). For the people, it was said that 'laws and regulations are in such confusion that the law that people have is difficult to follow' (Kuang-ming Jih-pao, 19 June 1957). As for the work on the draft criminal code, it was common to see the statement, 'Only the sound of footsteps is heard on the stairs and no one is seen descending' (e.g., Kuang-ming Jih-pao, 1 June 1957). Systematic reporting of case law, institutionalised in the Manchu Dynasty in the Hsing-an Hui-lan (Bodde and Morris, 1967: 203–542), remains unknown in the PRC. 'The data relating to judicial practice in our courts everywhere at every level under the present circumstances are very difficult for our people doing legal studies to obtain and so it is very difficult to make sufficient use of it', said a Hundred Flowers critic (Kuang-ming Jih-pao, 12 June 1957). From a substantive point of view, then, most criminal cases in the PRC have been decided without published guidance.

*Development of Procedural Law in the PRC*

The genius of the leadership of the Chinese Communist Party is well displayed in the formal organisational structure of the society (see Schurmann, 1969). The Constitution of 1954 and accompanying legislation established a judicial structure modelled on that of the

Soviet Union. Accompanying the courts are various levels of a procuracy. The police operate at the lowest level from public security stations which report ultimately to the State Council. Paralleling the official law-enforcement and judicial structure is a semi-official set of groups, the most noteworthy of which are the mediation committees. The overall structure is well depicted by Cohen (1968:139–141).

Mediation is a time-honoured practice in China (see Van der Sprenkel, 1962:97 *et seq.*). Much of the burden of handling offences has been given to mediation committees in the PRC (Cohen, 1968:25). In addition, everyone in the cities belongs to political groups at home and at work, and in the countryside everyone is in a small political organisation also, generally a production brigade. One receives the impression that most social conflicts are resolved by the lowest-level people's groups themselves under the guidance of Party cadres, without official involvement (see, e.g., Myrdal and Kessle, 1970). Yang (1972:19) noted the predominance of 'small group, social control' during his recent visit to cities and communes in China. This again reflects Chinese tradition (see Van der Sprenkel, 1962:97 *et seq.*). Of course, Party and Youth League members are subject to internal disciplinary procedures of their own (see Cohen, 1968:188–192).

The existence of such an elaborate control structure does not necessarily imply an institutionalised criminal law procedure, however. When substantive laws are applied in the PRC, they 'not infrequently are applied retroactively and analogically or, to put it most crudely, on an *ad hoc* basis' (Pfeffer, 1970:261). An attempt to develop an organised bar to protect the rights of the accused lasted a year or two and was cut short by the Anti-Rightist Movement (see Cohen, 1968:17). At the zenith of the development of procedural as well as substantive criminal law during the Hundred Flowers Period in 1957, critics were wont to remark on the irregularities of the legal process. An adviser to the Supreme People's Court complained that 'certain judicial personnel' could not distinguish between what was and was not a crime and passed arbitrary sentences (*Kuang-ming Jih-pao*, 10 June 1957). Criticism during the period was mainly of Party members' conduct, and it was said that a section of the Party leadership (shortly to predominate) maintained that it was 'only natural for the Party to take the place of the Government, that the Party's orders are above the law' (*Kuang-ming Jih-pao*, 25 May 1957, translated in MacFarquhar, 1960:129). The problem was not so much seen as being a dearth of procedural guidelines for use in criminal prosecution, but as one of the guidelines being ignored. Thus:

> The Party and the Government did give attention to the protection of citizens' rights, and Article 97 of the Constitution clearly provides that effective guarantee is to be made of those rights. But can the ordinary citizen who is dealt with under the work style of some basic-level cadres in which they issue harsh directives effectively exercise the right of appeal granted by the Constitution? Do the state organs make compensation in accord with the Constitution for all the injuries to citizen's rights caused by the cadres' illegal usurpations? It remains questionable. (*Kuang-ming Jih-pao*, 31 May 1957)

Hence, as far as can be seen, to this day in the PRC there is little regularity in the application of a criminal law of little substance.

*Role of the Principle of Legality: the American View*

It would be practically the unanimous view of American scholars of jurisprudence, of anthropology and of sociology of law that the evolution of the criminal law system in the PRC has been regressive. They would maintain that what little progress had been made in legal development in the PRC until 1957 was obliterated by the Anti-Rightest Movement. Selznick (1968:52) speaks for the American disciplines when he writes:

> In a developed legal order, authority transcends coercion, accepts the restraint of reason, and contributes to a public conscience regarding the foundations of civic obligation. To the extent that law is 'the enterprise of subjecting human conduct to the governance of rules' (Fuller, 1964:106), it can be said that law aims at a moral achievement. The name of that achievement is legality or 'the rule of law.' Its distinctive contribution is a progressive reduction of the arbitrary element in positive law and its administration.
>
> As an intellectual discipline, the sociology of law has a far broader compass than the study of 'the requirements of justice which lawyers term principles of legality' (Hart, 1961:202). Not

every society gives equal weight to the ideal of 'control by rule' as against other ideals; and there is much to be said about law in society. Still, law is so intimately associated with the realization of these special values that study of 'the rule of law' must be a chief preoccupation of legal sociology.

Clearly, the Party leadership in the PRC has opted to move away from development of the principle of legality or the rule of law as herein described by Selznick. In the conception of Hoebel (1954:293), an American anthropologist, the PRC would therefore be an evolutionary throwback. From the perspective of Fuller (1964:33−94), an American scholar of jurisprudence, it could not even be considered a legal system at all, for it has none of his eight elements definitive of a legal system's existence. To Parsons (1962:58−62), an American sociologist, the PRC would fail to have the legal system requisite to preventing itself from 'breaking down into overt or chronic conflict' as a social system. Each of these men would agree that a 'general function of law in any society is that of enabling members of the society to calculate the consequences of their conduct, thereby facilitating voluntary transactions and arrangements' (Berman and Greiner, 1966:31−33). A critic from the Hundred Flowers Period in the PRC also held this opinion:

> The people know that if the existence of their rights and duties is established and the limits of their freedom made clear, it can increase their sense of security. Because of this, the promulgation of the criminal law, the civil law, the criminal and civil procedural laws, etc., is a problem in urgent need of solution. (*Kuang-ming Jih-pao*, 1 May 1957)

For better or worse, those in political control in that critic's country have chosen to disagree.


*Role of the Principle of Legality: the Chinese Communist View*

Though it is manifest that the leadership of the PRC does not consider development of the principle of legality to be consistent with its goals of political and social development, explicit statements of rationale for this position are hard to find. In a speech to the National People's Congress signalling the beginning of the Anti-Rightist Movement, Chou En-lai stated:

> In the early days of the foundation of our state, and throughout the period of transition, political and economic conditions changed rapidly, and it was, and continues to be difficult to draw up laws of a fundamental character suited to long-term periods. For instance, it is difficult to draft the civil and criminal codes before the completion of the main or socialist transformation of the private ownership of the means of production and the full establishment of the socialist ownership of the means of production. (New China News Agency, 26 June 1957, translated in MacFarquhar, 1960:282)

Conversely, it can be inferred that the party leadership believes development of the principle of legality would support a bourgeois social system and impede revolutionary passage of the society into proletarian control. From a Marxist frame of reference, development of the principle of legality at this stage of social transformation in the PRC would support historical regression rather than positive evolution. Thus, the Chinese Communist position is antithetical to that of Western scholars of legal development.

By referring to Marxist doctrine and Maoist thought, a plausible explanation of the Party position on the development of the principle of legality is not difficult to construct. The revolution in the PRC operates on the Marxist premise that human emancipation can be obtained by the overthrow of the class of those who characteristically exploit others (the bourgeoisie) by the class of those characteristically exploited (the proletariat). Mao Tse-Tung expanded Marxist theory to provide an agrarian base for his revolution – the peasantry being included in the proletariat and landlords being considered bourgeois. Bringing an end to exploitation is a fundamental goal of the Maoist revolution.

Exploitation is seen as being reflected in any class structure. A person or group occupying a higher class position than another person or group of necessity does so at the expense of the lower class. In the Marxist and Maoist view, even social status differences in Weberian (1947:424–429) terms have economic or social class roots. Hence, any

83

social differentiation in the PRC indicates that the Maoist revolution has not been accomplished; all social differentiation must be eliminated.

From the time of his early writings, Marx showed an awareness that exploitative social differentiation has a psychological component. Writing about a condition (political emancipation) that accompanies a society dominated by the bourgeoisie, Marx said:

> Political emancipation is a reduction of man, on the one hand to a member of civil society, an *independent* and *egoistic* individual, and on the other hand, to a citizen, to a moral person.
>
> Human emancipation will only be complete when the real, individual man has absorbed into himself the abstract citizen; when as an individual man, in his everyday life, in his work, and in his relationships, he has become a *species-being* . . . (Marx, 1963:31)

The creative ability innate and common to every human being is the part of man which Marx considers the species-being. Though different men have different talents, the possession of this creative ability in any form is for Marx what exalts man. The appreciation of this quality — the consciousness that its presence alone regardless of its form makes all other human characteristics insignificant in assessing the worth of a person — together with the development of an environment conducive to each man's enjoying (but not necessarily owning) the fruits of his own and others' shared talent, represents for Marx the escape from alienation and into human emancipation. When a man develops a consciousness of his existence as a species-being, he has no basis for making social differentiation psychologically, then. The man who lives as a species-being lives in a world without class or status of social significance to him.

Mao and his associates have recognised that the alienated proletarian who assumes political power does not automatically derive the consciousness of an unalienated species-being. In a real sense, Mao has turned Marx on his head. Rather than holding that a revolution in economic and political relations would in itself result in a revolution in the consciousness of the ruling class, Mao and his associates have held that a revolution must occur in the consciousness of the masses before the revolution in economic and political relations can be secured.

This view is reflected in a 1939 speech by Liu Shao-ch'i to Party members on how to lead the revolution. In the speech, entitled 'On the Cultivation of a Communist', he began:

> Comrades! In order to become the best and most faithful pupils of Marx, Engels, Lenin and Stalin, we need to carry on cultivation in every regard in the course of the long and great revolutionary struggle of the proletariat and masses of the people. We need to carry on cultivation in the theories of Marxism-Leninism and in applying such theories in practice; cultivation in revolutionary strategy and tactics; cultivation in studying and dealing with various problems according to the standpoint of Marxism-Leninism; cultivation in ideology and moral character; cultivation in Party unity, intra-Party struggle and discipline; cultivation in hard work and in the style of work; cultivation in being skillful in dealing with different kinds of people and in associating with the masses of the people; cultivation in various kinds of scientific knowledge, etc. We are all Communist Party members and so we have a general cultivation in common. But there exists a wide discrepancy today among our Party members. Wide discrepancy exists among us in the levels of political consciousness, in work, in position, in cultural level, in experience of struggle and in social origin. Therefore, in addition to cultivation in general we also need special cultivation for different groups and for individual comrades.

Even today, those at the vanguard of the revolution, let alone the masses of the proletariat, need to work to refine their consciousness. Correct action flows from correct thought.

The basic psychological impediment standing in the way of the development of a proletarian consciousness is individualism — the identity that carries with it an acceptance of social differentiation. 'In short, individualism is the source of all evils' (Lin, 1960:88). It is reasonable to assume that the leadership in the PRC has refused to develop the principle of legality primarily because it would support the development and maintenance of one's identity as an individual within the new social order.

Recall that a Hundred Flowers critic called for development of the substantive criminal and civil law in the PRC in order that people's 'sense of security' might be increased (*Kuang-ming Jih-pao*, 1 May 1957). Security in the face of the collective as represented by the state may well be a reinforcement of one's individuality, however. If I know the limits of my duties toward others in my society, it can readily be inferred that these limits will define the extent of my identification with those others. A Marxist consciousness, on the other hand, requires that the totality of thinking and feeling that guides my social action be founded on my existence as a species-being — on my acceptance of the inseparability of my socially significant qualities from what I share with all men. If I am to have a Marxist consciousness in *all* that I do I must be guided by what benefits all men undifferentiatedly as against what benefits myself alone. 'Everything for the public; nothing for the private (*ta-kung wu-szu*)', demands a Party slogan. What motivates all my action is a collective will; the expression of an individual will is an alienated and exploitative expression. The resocialisation into the consciousness that will bring the revolution to fruition thus requires that I accept the limitlessness of collective demands upon me — that I never feel entitled as a matter of right to stand against the collective or its representative, the state as a socially distinct entity. To raise the argument from a psychological to an institutional level, human emancipation must be accompanied by an end to the institution of private ownership, which the principle of legality defends as a personal right to life, liberty or property.

This would appear to be the reason that, to the leadership in the PRC, support for the principle of legality implies support for individualism and exploitation. Such support would stand in the way of a communist revolution. The refusal of the leadership in the PRC to develop the principle of legality may actually have facilitated progress toward the attainment of Marxist human emancipation in that country. A direct connection is difficult to draw at such a distance, but it is worth hypothesising about the relationship between the use of law in the PRC and an observation of Yang's (1972:19) about the social change he saw in the country:

> The most important change may be in the form of the remaking of the Chinese personality to fit the ideological schemes of the Socialist order. The Chinese we encountered are quite different from the Chinese in traditional days in that they are now highly politically conscious, morally puritanical, deeply aware of national and collective goals, and above all organized and disciplined as a population.

*The Principle of Legality and Individualism*

The experience in the PRC implies a relationship between legal structure and life among a general populace:

> *The development of the principle of legality in a society will promote the recognition of individualistic accomplishment by that society's members, while societal movement away from the principle of legality will promote the recognition of collective accomplishment.*

Individualistic accomplishment is a product of social action with which an individual is identified. It would be recognised in statements like, 'Under John Doe's administration the standard of living improved considerably', or, 'Joe Smith invented a new irrigation technique', or, 'Charles Entrepreneur made his first million dollars by the time he was thirty years old'. Collective accomplishment, on the other hand, is a product of social action with which a group is identified. It would be recognised in such statements as, 'through a well-coordinated effort with broad community participation, the standard of living in the city of Metropolis increased considerably', or, 'the production team at Green Acres developed a new irrigation technique', or, 'the residents of Workers' Commune increased their level of production five-fold in their first three years of operation'. Both forms of expression are likely to be found in any large society, but the form of the legal system theoretically should give the one form predominance over the other.

The association between the development of the principle of legality and the promotion of individualism can be translated from Marxist and Maoist theoretical terms into more characteristically American language. As the discussion above of the predominant American view of the importance of the principle of legality indicates, the institutionalisation of the principle is seen to facilitate voluntary transactions and arrangements by enabling members of a society to calculate the consequences of their conduct. This implies that risk is a factor in an individual's decision as to whether to permit himself to become personally recognised as having taken a course of action. The state in its substantive and procedural laws can lessen the risk by telling the individual how societal instruments of justice can be marshalled to support or negatively sanction what he or she does. The individual can then select some actions to take which he or she can assume at the very least will not result in state-imposed punishment. A person may in many cases even be able to call on state force to protect him or her from adverse private reactions to what he or she does. Further, having acted, the person will have a measure of security in claiming or accepting personal recognition for what he has done.

Conversely, as apparently is true in the PRC, the individual actor may have little or no indication as to what kind of personal action may result in a favourable or unfavourable state response. Such is apt to be the case where development of the principle of legality is successfully resisted in a society. The individual in this situation is still likely to have to take courses of action visible to others. Even retreat from public view could become such a visible course of action. Assuming still that the individual will try to minimise the risk of punishment by the state and to maximise the probability of state protection for his or her deeds, he or she must choose a strategy of action different from that where the principle of legality is developed. The person will not be apt to want personal recognition for his or her acts; the danger such recognition carries is too great. If, on the other hand, the person can help to establish the notion that his or her actions are not significantly different from those of neighbouring others, such a form of social anonymity may be his or her best protection. If anything significant is accomplished, the individual will be safest if the responsibility for the accomplishment is attached to a group as a whole rather than to individuals in it. The security of the suppression of individual identity may best be obtained by contributing to the collective identification with others. This being the optimal strategy for all actors in a social system moving away from the principle of legality, the members of the society generally should tend to give recognition to collective rather than individualistic accomplishment.

For some societies, evolution may be in the direction of increased recognition for individualistic accomplishment. Here the typically American premise about legal development would hold true. In other societies, such as a Marxist-oriented one in which individualism is a symbol of anachronistic oppression, evolution may require that the development of the principle of legality be suppressed. It remains to be seen which other popular behaviour patterns might be implied by such a choice.

NOTES

1. Thanks are given for permission to adapt this chapter from the present author's article, 'The people v. the principle of legality in the People's Republic of China', *Journal of Criminal Justice*, 1 (March): 51—60.
2. The development of law and legal institutions in the PRC is thoroughly covered in Cohen (1968). This section and the next are essentially short restatements of the same material.

REFERENCES

Berman, Harold J., and William R. Greiner. 1966. *The Nature and Functions of Law*. Brooklyn: Foundations Press (2nd edn).
Bodde, Derk, and Clarence Morris. 1967. *Law in Imperial China*. Cambridge, Mass.: Harvard University Press.
Cohen, Jerome A. 1968. *The Criminal Process in the People's Republic of China: 1949—1963*. Cambridge, Mass.: Harvard University Press.
Fuller, Lon L. 1964. *The Morality of Law*. New Haven, Connecticut: Yale University Press.
Hart, H. L. A. 1961. *The Concept of Law*. Oxford: Clarendon Press.
Hoebel, E. Adamson. 1954. *The Law of Primitive Man: A Study in Comparative Legal Dynamics*. Cambridge, Mass.: Harvard University Press.
*Kuang-ming Jih-pao* (The Enlightenment Daily). Peking.
Lin Piao. 1960. 'March ahead under the red flag of the Party's general line and Mao Tse-Tung's military thinking', in *Ten Glorious Years*, pp. 86—90. Peking: Foreign Languages Press.
MacFarquhar, Roderick. 1960. *The Hundred Flowers*. London: Stevens Press.
Marx, Karl (T. B. Bottomore, ed. and trans.). 1963. 'Bruno Bauer, die Judenfrage', in *Karl Marx: Early Writings*, pp. 3—31. New York: McGraw-Hill.
Myrdal, Jan, and Gun Kessle (Paul B. Austin, trans.). 1970. *China: The Revolution Continued*. New York: Pantheon Books.
Parsons, Talcott. 1962. 'The law and social control', in William M. Evan (ed.), *Law and Sociology: Exploratory Essays*, pp. 56—72. New York: Free Press.
Pfeffer, Richard M. 1970. 'Crime and punishment: China and the United States', in Jerome A. Cohen, *Contemporary Chinese Law: Problems and Perspectives*, pp. 261—281. Cambridge, Mass.: Harvard University Press.
Rosenberg, Milton J., and Robert P. Abelson. 1960. 'An analysis of cognitive balancing', in Milton J. Rosenberg, Carl I. Hovland, William J. McGuire, Robert P. Abelson and Jack W. Brenner (eds), *Attitude Organization and Change: An Analysis of Consistency Among Attitude Components*, pp. 112—163. New Haven: Yale University Press.
Rothman, David J. 1971. *The Discovery of the Asylum: Social Order and Disorder in the New Republic*. Boston: Little, Brown and Company.
Schurmann, H. Franz. 1969. *Ideology and Organization in Communist China*. Berkeley: University of California Press (2nd edn).
Selznick, Philip. 1968. 'The sociology of law', in David Sills (ed.), *International Encyclopedia of the Social Sciences*, Vol. 9, pp. 50—59. New York: Macmillan and Free Press.

Van der Sprenkel, Sybille. 1962. *Legal Institutions in Manchu China*. London: Athlone Press.

Weber, Max (Talcott Parsons, ed. and trans.). 1947. *The Theory of Social and Economic Organization*. New York: Free Press.

Yang, C. K. 1972. 'C. K. Yang, first U.S. sociologist to visit China'. *American Sociologist*, 7 (July): 1,19.

## 6. CONSTRAINTS ON THE GENERAL POPULACE: LEGAL PROTECTION OF THE RIGHT TO SOCIAL MOBILITY[1]

*Introduction*

On the surface, application of the Chinese form of legal system may appear clearly and simply to be repressive. Not surprisingly, in the United States the practical absence of utilised formal written law is generally viewed as a fearsome prospect (except to a few commentators, such as Quinney, 1972). The threat of repression is commonly held to be foreboding enough, even if, as is apparently the case in the People's Republic of China (PRC) today, it is rare to find someone actually 'punished according to law'. The threat of political repression is not all that is aversive about the thought of a curtailing of reliance on formal written law. The prospect of a breakdown of social order, of rampant social conflict, of anarchy is also foreseen (although a simultaneous state of anarchy and state repression is evidently paradoxical). Conversely, reliance on a formal written law is seen to restrict both each citizen's freedom to act uncontrolled by the demands of others and others' freedom to control each citizen's freedom of action. This view is also paradoxical. Each notion implies that citizens' freedom from control by agents of the state co-varies directly with state agents' control of citizens' freedom of action. The paradoxes are eliminated only by making logically tenable the possibility of a simultaneous increase and decrease in citizens' freedom from control by state agents, accompanied by a simultaneous decrease and increase in state agents' control of citizens' freedom of action.

It is therefore possible that Americans' typical visions of the consequences of lesser reliance on formal written law might be qualifiedly valid. In one sense, freedom of citizens' actions from control by state agents might be increased, while in another sense it would be decreased. The way in which persons' freedom would be increased and that in which it would be restricted remain to be projected.

91

Indications are that commitment to maintaining particular relationships is lower in the United States than in the People's Republic of China. Commitment as here used is the probability that social relationships with the same persons will be maintained over time.

Social statistics are easier to obtain in the USA than in the PRC, though ordinal comparisons between the two polities remain possible. To begin with, geographical mobility is higher in the USA than in the PRC. One fifth of all Americans move from one residence to another each year (see Simmons, 1968:622). In China, one lives where assigned. Unauthorised and authorised movement from countryside to cities are both apparently kept infrequent in a predominantly rural country. Most of those who are sent to the countryside are sent only temporarily to learn the meaning of working with the masses, though some stay in the countryside for long periods of time. Community members sent to cities are generally sent temporarily for education and training to use back at home. To be sure, a number of Chinese are permanently assigned to work far away from their homes. However, the rate of geographical mobility, especially from one neighbourhood to the next in the same metropolitan area, appears to be far higher in the USA than in the PRC.

Occupational mobility is rather high in the USA if one includes horizontal mobility as well as the less frequent vertical mobility. The latest American data on frequency of job change are unfortunately rather old (from 1949), but there is no reason to believe that frequency of job change has decreased since that time. The findings, by Lipset and Bendix (1959) in Oakland, showed unskilled workers having held an average of more than ten jobs. Business managers and executives, at the other extreme, had averaged over three jobs apiece. The overall average number of jobs held by all those sampled was 6.3.

The rate of change of occupation would have to be lower than the rate of change of jobs, but even in this category only 29.3 per cent of American males between the ages of 25 and 64 were found not to have changed occupations as of 1962 (US Bureau of the Census, 1964).

Apparently, in the PRC occupational mobility is minimal. Once trained, urban workers are reported to change jobs either only as a job is eliminated in favour of another or temporarily from managerial status to work among the masses. Rural workers may perform different jobs as local needs change, such as from cultivating to harvesting of crops or to construction of irrigation facilities. Very much like the small American farmer, the rural Chinese is apt to be more a generalist than a specialist. However, the work setting is not apt to change for the rural resident.

Hence, at home and at work, Chinese tend to stay with the same people far longer than their American counterparts.

While divorce is rather commonplace and ever easier to obtain in the USA, divorce is seemingly rather difficult to obtain in the PRC since the Cultural Revolution (in the late sixties). Lubman (1973) describes a divorce trial he attended in Peking. The district judge went to the tractor factory where the estranged husband and wife worked. He 'had already interviewed husband and wife singly and together as well as their neighbours, fellow workers and supervisors. All past attempts to keep them together had failed, however, and the wife had persisted in her demand for a divorce'.

The judge interviewed the couple singly and together once again. With him were a group of the couples' neighbours and fellow workers, or 'masses' representatives'. Duties under two of the few laws in the PRC, the Constitution of 1954 and the Marriage Law of 1950, were vaguely described – to 'mutually love and respect each other' and to 'participate in Socialist construction'. The husband had committed adultery and had struck his wife in a quarrel, but these were considered past problems to be overcome in a reconciliation, not grounds for a separation. Following the counsel of the 'masses' representatives', the judge ordered the husband to sign a 'statement of guarantee' that he would not again strike his wife. Failure to keep the guarantee would ostensibly be grounds for a divorce and injury to the wife would result in 'punishment according to law' (threatening, but remote). The representatives would continue to 're-educate' the husband and 'assist' in the reconciliation process. Lubman concludes, 'The trial expressed the ideal of Chinese justice – to avoid formal adjudication of disputes between citizens and to strengthen the social solidarity of the working class'.

Professor Victor Li of Stanford University Law School had a similar reconciliation attempt described to him during a visit to the PRC. Apparently, a husband had constantly been late to work and was making mistakes on the job. His work group had asked him for an explanation. He replied that he and his wife were fighting because they

93

saw so little of each other so that he was losing sleep and could not focus on his work. The wife worked another shift at the same plant. The group sent the husband's supervisor to the wife's supervisor to arrange for the husband and wife to work on the same shift. The husband was exhorted to study his mistakes and improve his work.

Two contrasts in domestic relations with the USA are noteworthy. First, much greater emphasis in the PRC than in the USA (with parades of faceless people moving through routine and often uncontested divorce hearings) is put on keeping spouses together in the same relationship. For a spouse simply to abandon a family would be inconceivable in the PRC. Second, one's co-workers and supervisors get much more thoroughly involved in the intimate details of a person's home life than would characteristically be the case in the USA.

As Cohen (1968) describes, groups and mediation mechanisms exist for residents of urban areas similar to those for workers. 'Mediation' is something of a misnomer, for it is practically unheard of for disputants not to defer to the counsel of their 'mediators', though the process lacks the formal written guarantees of authority of what we know as arbitration. The point is that reconciliation and persuasion will be tried repeatedly and with involvement of many familiar faces at work and in the neighbourhood before the disputants may be released from the burden of trying to resolve their differences within ongoing relationships.

Extended observations of the police (Pepinsky, 1972:72—78), corroborated by police officers from various parts of the country, have suggested that the situation in US urban neighbourhoods is different. A large portion of citizen complaints to patrolmen call for the patrolmen to act as the citizens' agents in resolving petty problems with relatives and neighbours. One common complaint, especially in apartment buildings, is that neighbours are playing music too loudly. Usually, in these cases, the complainant has not approached his neighbour directly and stays away while the police convey his demand. The complainant is apt not even to know the neighbour. Other common complaints would be of neighbours parking in front of the complainant's home, of neighbours' children or pets causing minor damage or simply a disturbance on the complainant's property, of landlords locking tenants out of apartments or rooms, of alcoholic or infirm elderly neighbours or family needing removal (somewhat like garbage), or of petty but voluble family arguments. The police may not enjoy being called upon to handle such problems, but in practice generally concur in the wisdom of their separating the disputants. The police also generally consider it good practice to end their own involvement as rapidly as possible, believing that the most they can do is to cool down the conflict of the moment.

Citizen complaints to police exemplify the source of a second type of mobility far more commonly found in the USA than in the PRC. Not only are American citizens more apt to move from one place of residence or work to the next and to do so at will, but Americans in a number of cases use third persons to take care of (removing, if necessary) people with whom Americans get into conflict in residence situations. According to Rothman (1971:57–59), both forms of mobility became salient simultaneously in the Jacksonian era in the USA. The American does not rely solely on removing himself from others; he can have the others removed or restrained while he remains aloof from them, and, literally, relatively unmoved himself. Characteristically, a Chinese would not be permitted to absolve himself or herself of responsibility for carrying on relationships with family and neighbours throughout periods of conflict and need. The Chinese can remove himself or herself, or others, from troublesome situations only rarely, and then in the guise and with the consensus of comrades that in the overall task of Socialist construction the person is more valuable elsewhere.

Commonly, juveniles who are institutionalised in the USA are so treated because they have caused trouble in school (see Newman, 1972). Cicourel and Kitsuse (1968) have described the process by which troublemakers in American schools get picked out and isolated from their peers. Contrast this with the report that in the PRC 'a MS (middle school) class receives the grade of its poorest achiever' (Yee, 1973:12). Frank criticism of others and of oneself, as a prelude to reintegration of a 'deviant' back into a group, and continuing to help someone who is not making his fair contribution to do so, are acceptable ways of handling social conflict and disruption, but in school and elsewhere isolation of a person would seldom be considered a viable solution to any problem. If anything, the opposite tends to be the case, for a person causing trouble is considered to require more rather than less intensive interaction with and attention from his peers. In general, while stress is conventionally associated with mobility in the USA (See Clark and Cadwallader, 1973), stress is conventionally

95

associated with 'criticism' and 'struggle' in the PRC.

This set of examples indicates consistently a greater tendency in the USA for citizens to move among relationships than is the case in the PRC. Presumably, too, there is more occasion for citizens to express themselves in private, as by painting, alone, than would be the case in the PRC, where all action is to be public. The right to privacy has in fact been held to be implicit in law as law is known in the USA (United States Supreme Court, 1965). On the other hand, PRC citizens seem more consistently to stay involved in ongoing relationships through problem situations than do their US counterparts. As a result, the scope of the relationships in the PRC appears characteristically to extend beyond that of corresponding relationships in the USA.

Hence, the state which restricts less – and even encourages – social mobility is also the one that relies more heavily on formal written law.

The freedom more typical for Chinese than for Americans is difficult to describe. It is a kind of freedom with which Americans are largely unfamiliar. For Americans this freedom has a subtlety corresponding to its salience for the Chinese. The freedom is that of developing access to new economic and social resources within the context of existing relationships.

The improvement in the economic lot of the average Chinese over the last twenty-five years is dramatic and well known. Where famines periodically took millions of lives, all people have enough to eat. All in the cities have shelter, where many once had only the streets on which to live. Middle-school education has become universal where illiteracy was the norm. Myrdal and Kessle (1970:52–55) found that through collective effort the 'five guarantees' of enough food, enough fuel, health care, an honourable funeral and education for the children had become a reality for everyone even in a relatively poor village in Yenan in 1969. Myrdal and Kessle provide perhaps the most detailed, vivid and credible description of the form of the collective effort in the PRC.

However, for those accustomed to relative affluence, as in the USA, any description of collective accomplishment in the PRC is apt to seem trivial. The general strength of interpersonal competition has become an American assumption. The following scenario has been developed to translate the recent Chinese experience into an American context.

The US President has just made a nationwide television address telling Americans of a fuel crisis and asking them to curtail petrol consumption as much as possible. No formal action is contemplated;

full faith is being placed in the voluntary cooperation of the citizenry, in accord with the political ideology that has become nationally dominant in recent years.

Outside the city of Gotham, at the 2100 block of Rich Street in the suburb of Pleasantview, darkness has fallen. It is 8:00 — time for the nightly block meeting. Jack and Doris Stormann generally host the meeting in their spacious home. Tonight is no exception.

Almost everyone has arrived. The children are being watched tonight by Dan and Barbara Spinoza, who are taking their turn in the babysitting rotation. In the living room, about thirty people are sitting in a circle — each already engaged with his neighbours in discussion of the President's speech. Conversation among them is relaxed, for most of them have known each other, in and out of these meetings, for years. Then block chairperson Mary Geller, bearing in mind that her responsibility is to elicit a cooperative response to the fuel crisis, calls the meeting to order.

'Obviously, the President's speech is in all our minds', she begins. 'Anyone who wants to comment on it may speak.'

'Apparently, the fuel crisis is real. We simply have to use our cars a lot less than we've been doing.' Heads nod in agreement. Bill Samuels has expressed a preliminary consensus of the meeting.

Discussion moves quickly to the ways in which members of the group can help one another to meet the agreed objective. Use of the bus service is suggested, but a number of disparaging remarks about the service lead to abandonment of this idea.

Then a member of the group raises the notion of a car pool. A car pool is acceptable to everyone but George Jones, who likes to be alone on the way to work. 'How can you be so selfish in a matter of such importance?' he is asked. George argues a while for his conception of his rights, but eventually his resistance gives way to assent. Even if he had left the meeting to escape the group pressure, he soon would have been visited by a delegation seeking to 'help' him with 'his problem'. It has come to be taken for granted by all participants that no one can expect to get away with pursuit of private interests in matters of public concern.    And so it is agreed that eight car pools will be established to take the neighbours to and from places of work in various areas of the community. The membership of each pool is established, and each pool is asked to work out its own schedule, rotation of driving and plan for sharing expenses.

Then it is noted that a substantial number of housewives in the neighbourhood have shopping to do and other errands to run. With little deliberation, the notion of car pools is extended to meet these needs. On a rotating schedule, individual housewives accept the responsibility for taking calls from those who plan to go out during the day. The first to call who has use of a car and who cannot make use of transport in a car already scheduled to go on a trip is to be a driver, and the coordinator of the day refers subsequent callers to her as passengers. Also on a rotating basis, two housewives a day are enlisted for child care while both parents are away. Thus, mothers and fathers are freed from having to take small children with them on their various trips. Such a child care programme has already been tried and proven for evening babysitting. Children have learned to look forward to staying even overnight with neighbours as a kind of adventure. From previous experience, any inequities in allocation of responsibilities versus utilisation of services are left to be adjusted as they arise in future meetings.

The meeting has been going on for nearly an hour. By convention, it is about time to adjourn. Alice Ladinsky mentions that she and her husband have been having marital difficulties, and asks leave to discuss them in the next meeting. Her husband, Mark, concurs. Without objection, the chairperson approves the request. The meeting is over.

Over the years, the need for social services in the block has declined markedly. The police have not been called for the past two years. A few would-be burglars have been scared off by watchful neighbours. Loans have been arranged by the group for families in a financial crisis. Members of the group have effectively acted as informal therapists for one another. The rate of movement in and out of the neighbourhood has declined to insignificance, for the social support provided there has proved generally more valuable to the residents than occupational mobility.

The scenario is designed to highlight the kind of freedom offered by a social system geared to collective accomplishment rather than to social mobility. It is closely modelled on accounts of group activity in the PRC, such as those by Myrdal and Kessle (1970). The cooperative effort of a stable group (or groups) provides opportunities and services closely tuned to the needs of the members. Each member has a freedom to choose among services that would otherwise be unavailable or not so well suited to his or her requirements. In the process of restricting social mobility by organising people into groups, and, initially at least, of trying to enforce members' participation in them, the role of the state in providing rules and institutions especially for conflict resolution and provision of services tends to become superfluous. The kind of individual freedom from control by state agents changes as one moves from a social system relying heavily on formal written law to one resisting such reliance. However, the overall quantum of freedom cannot be shown to differ between the two systems.

*Impact on the General Populace*

Weber (1967:5) has translated the meaning of law, including its formal written form, into functional terms:

> An order will be called *law* if it is externally guaranteed by the probability that coercion (physical or psychological), to bring about conformity or average violation, will be applied by a *staff* of people holding themselves specially ready for that purpose.

When a law is formal and written, the law carries the additional promise that the order of coercion is knowable in advance and that the probability of coercion is linked to the knowable order. Commitment to formal written law by members of society seems to imply logically that 'a general function of law in any society is that of enabling members of the society to calculate the consequences of their conduct, thereby securing and facilitating voluntary transactions and arrangements' (Berman and Greiner, 1966:31).

As the system of formal written law serves this function of creating security, it engenders a dependence by the society's members and thereby restricts their freedom of action. As long ago as 1840, de Tocqueville (1956:303–304) found a role for formal written law in a kind of despotism which he foresaw coming to the USA. He wrote:

> (Despotism) covers the surface of society with *a network of small, complicated rules, minute and uniform*, through which the most original minds and the most energetic characters cannot penetrate, to rise above the crowd. The will of man is not shattered, but

99

ᴇMORY & HENRY LIBRARY

softened, bent, and guided; men are seldom forced by it to act, but they are constantly restrained from acting: such a power does not destroy, but it prevents existence; it does not tyrannize, but it compresses, enervates, and stupifies a people, till each nation is reduced to nothing better than a pack of animals, of which the government is the shepherd. (Italics added)

There has been a tendency to analogise exhortations in newspapers, on radio and in Party directives in the PRC to the formal written law in the USA. There is a significant difference between the published exhortations in the PRC and the terms of the law in the USA, however. The exhortations in the PRC contain three elements: (a) statements of what social products are needed from collective actions (e.g. the level of industrial output must be increased), (b) descriptions of tools that can be used by groups to shape social action to obtain the products (e.g. criticism and persuasion), and (c) specification of attitudes or general approaches to action which are obstacles to production (e.g. bureaucratism). Attempts at formal statements of what particular products of action are required from *individuals* have been practically abandoned since the disaster of the 'Great Leap Forward' programme in the late 1950s, when it proved ineffective, for instance, to set quotas on production of pig iron by individuals in backyard furnaces. Official pronouncements in the PRC prescribe *how* individual conduct is to be decided upon within community groups. Official pronouncements do not designate *what* each individual's conduct shall be.

The formal written law of the USA, on the other hand, predominately prescribes *what* conduct is required by individuals. Indeed, the US Supreme Court has held that the criminal law, as law is traditionally conceived, can only address concrete acts by people (United States Supreme Court, 1962). The 'rules' to which de Tocqueville refers are those which prescribe specific acts that an individual must or must not carry out. Rules of substantive conduct take decisions as to courses of action toward others out of the hands of individuals, while directives as to how and why decisions must be made place responsibility for these decisions squarely in the hands of the citizen, while tending to take away responsibility for when and where the decisions are made.

Experience in the USA and the PRC suggests two modifications of the role of rules — including those in formal written law. First, people are not restrained by use of the rules from moving among relationships

100

with others; they are encouraged to do so. Second, the restraint takes the form of providing a structural substitute for reliance on others for cooperation.

Reliance on formal written law reinforces a distrust of interpersonal support from particular people. The structure provided by rules indicates that the state through its agents will take care of the arrangements of interpersonal relations where these relations are necessary. People are seen as trouble; the only thing they characteristically can and will provide not supplied by the legal order is capricious, unpredictable obstinacy and resistance to the furthering of one's personal interests. Associations with others tend to become those of momentary convenience. When another stands in one's way, it is best to move along.

By its explicit emphasis on the ordering of acts rather than the ordering of status, American formal written law replaces the attempted definition of where one is with that of what one does. Consistently, American formal written law even stresses a freedom of movement for its citizens. So long as the citizens do as the law commands, they are free to do it wherever they please. With its invitation to citizens to enjoy one kind of freedom, the American form of law helps discourage them from attempting to enjoy another.

The promulgation of formal written law dampens efforts to collective accomplishment in other ways, too. Such promulgation helps establish the conventional wisdom that the substance of appropriate and inappropriate action tends to be immutable and unvaried from one relationship and situation to the next. The idea that one can customarily create a novel form of action to meet the demands of a particular situation, changing the form in the next situation merely by the exercise of personal judgement, tends to be met with considerable scepticism.

By contrast, the system in which use of formal written law is eschewed essentially requires just one rule. The citizen shall stay with the group or groups in which he is placed by agents of the state. To some extent, agents of the state may also be relied on for information as to what social needs and problems are, and for feedback as to whether the needs are being met and the problems resolved. However, agents of the state tend to refrain from promulgating rules as to what each citizen is to do to work to meet even those needs and resolve the problems the agents attempt to define. The individual is restricted from moving among relationships, and forced to rely for survival on the relationships he or she is given. Survival seemingly requires that the individual be resourceful, adaptable and innovative in choosing a form of action to meet the demands of the moment.

In chapter 5, a theoretical basis was offered for an ideological preference for either the Chinese or the American form of legal system over the other. While theoretically better suited to rewarding individual accomplishment, the American legal system in practice seems also to reinforce various forms of social mobility and interpersonal competition and distrust. While theoretically better suited to rewarding collective accomplishment, the Chinese legal system in practice seems also to reinforce both commitment to maintenance of particular social relationships and interpersonal cooperation and trust. Both logically and empirically, the theoretical strengths of each legal system imply a set of behavioural responses among the general populace of subjects.

## Conclusion

There is, to say the least, scant indication that popular reliance on American law is on the wane. The number of lawyers in the USA is growing exponentially. New legislation is frequently and conventionally seen as the major tool needed to respond to domestic crises such as that known under the rubric of 'Watergate' and the energy crisis.

The argument here is that *if* attenuation of reliance on formal written law should occur in American society, the change would not occur in isolation. It is projected that any such attenuation would be accompanied by a change in the form of individual freedom from control by state agents that predominates in American society. American use of formal written law does not preserve *social order*; it is integrally linked to preservation of *a* social order. It does not preserve or establish *individual freedom* from social control by state agents; it is integrally tied to establishment or maintenance of *one form* of individual freedom at the expense of enjoyment of another form. It appears that it is overly simplistic to associate a reluctance to use formal written law with 'dictatorship' (as does Nagel, 1962) or to call a failure to adhere to the terms of formal written law 'undemocratic' (as does Evan, 1962). There is more than one way in which people can rule

102

themselves without some kind of state interference, and in the process of availing themselves of one kind of self-rule a people must give up another.

It now becomes possible to relate the response to formal written criminal law by American administrators to that by the general populace. While those who administer the law are constrained to participate discriminatively in a system of appropriation — in a competition for private property rights — the structure of the legal system discourages the populace from participating cooperatively in a collective utilisation of economic and personal resources. Instead, each member of the American populace tends to view his or her interests as antagonistic to those of others. The conception of interpersonal relations embodied in the criminal law tends to generalise to purportedly extra-legal affairs, reinforcing the view that what one person enjoys or obtains must be at another's expense. The system of appropriation, therefore, not only encompasses administration of the criminal law but tends to pervade interpersonal relations in the social system. What Bonger (1969) termed 'egoism' and saw as the underlying source of crime itself, what MacPherson (1962) has called 'possessive individualism' and traced to seventeenth-century English thought, what Weber (1958) called 'the spirit of capitalism' and traced to the rise of Calvinism, and what Arieli (1964) has traced to particularly American nationalism: this approach to life tends to predominate among the American populace. A relatively high rate of social mobility reflects the movement of persons from one appropriative relationship to the next, while supporting escape from interpersonal conflict rather than resolution of the conflict in ongoing relationships.

Since reliance on formal written law seems to reinforce the predominance of competitive over cooperative relationships in the American social system, the proposition would seem to follow that reliance on formal written law reinforces action that is deemed to constitute crime, as Bonger (1969) would suggest. The tenability of this proposition bears further scrutiny, which it is given in chapter 7.

# NOTES

1. Thanks are given for permission to adapt this chapter from the present author's article, 'Reliance on formal written law, and freedom and social control, in the United States and the People's Republic of China', *British Journal of Sociology*, 26 (September 1975): 330–342.

# REFERENCES

Arieli, Yekoshua. 1964. *Individualism and Nationalism in American Ideology.* Cambridge, Mass.: Harvard University Press.

Berman, Harold J. and William R. Greiner. 1966. *The Nature and Functions of Law.* Brooklyn: Foundation Press (2nd edn).

Bonger, Willem (Austin Turk, ed.). 1969. *Criminality and Economic Conditions.* Bloomington: Indiana University Press.

Cicourel, Aaron V., and John I. Kitsuse. 1968. 'The social organization of the high school and deviant adolescent careers', in Earl Rubington and Martin S. Weinberg, *Deviance: The Interactionist Perspective*, pp. 124–135. New York: Macmillan Company.

Clark, W. A. V., and Martin Cadwallader. 1973. 'Locational stress and residential mobility'. *Environment and Behavior*, 5 (March):29–41.

Cohen, Jerome A. 1968. *The Criminal Process in the People's Republic of China: 1949–1963.* Cambridge, Mass.: Harvard University Press.

Evan, William M. 1962. 'Public and private legal systems', in William M. Evan (ed.), *Law and Sociology: Exploratory Essays*, pp. 170–179. New York: Free Press.

Lipset, Seymour M., and Reinhard Bendix. 1959. *Social Mobility in Industrial Society.* Berkeley: University of California Press.

Lubman, Stanley. 1973. 'A divorce trial – Peking style'. *Wall Street Journal* (5 June):22.

MacPherson, C. B. 1962. *The Political Theory of Possessive Individualism.* London: Oxford University Press.

Myrdal, Jan, and Gun Kessle (Paul B. Austin, trans.). 1970. *China: The Revolution Continued.* New York: Pantheon Books.

Nagel, Stuart S. 1962. 'Culture patterns and judicial systems'. *Vanderbilt Law Review*, 16 (December):147–157.

Newman, Graeme R. 1972. *Deviance and Removal.* Philadelphia: University of Pennsylvania (dissertation).

Pepinsky, Harold E. 1972. *Police Decisions to Report Offenses.* Philadelphia: University of Pennsylvania (dissertation).

Quinney, Richard. 1972. 'The Ideology of Law: notes for a radical alternative to legal oppression'. *Issues in Criminology*, 7 (Winter):1–35.

Rothman, David J. 1971. *The Discovery of the Asylum: Social Order and Disorder in the New Republic.* Boston: Little, Brown and Company.

Simmons, James W. 1968. 'A review of interurban mobility'. *Geographical Review*, 58 (October):622–657.

Tocqueville, Alexis de (Richard D. Heffner, ed.). 1956. *Democracy in America.* New York: New American Library.

United States Bureau of the Census. 1964. 'Lifetime occupational mobility of adult males, March, 1962'. *Current Population Reports*, series P-23, no. 11 (May).

United States Supreme Court. 1962. *Robinson v. California*. 370 U.S. 660.

United States Supreme Court. 1965. *Griswold v. Connecticut*. 381 U.S. 479.

Weber, Max (Talcott Parsons, trans., with a foreword by R. H. Tawney). 1958. *The Protestant Ethic and the Spirit of Capitalism*. New York: Charles Scribner's Sons.

Weber, Max (Max Rheinstein, ed., and Edward Shils and Max Rheinstein, trans.). 1967. *Max Weber on Law in Economy and Society*. New York: Simon and Schuster.

Yee, Albert H. 1973. 'Schools and progress in the People's Republic of China'. *Educational Researcher*, 2 (July):5–15.

# 7.  AMERICAN  CRIMINAL  LAW'S CONTRIBUTION TO CRIME

## Introduction

It has already been established that maintenance of the American form of criminal law is symbiotically tied to predominant social acceptance of competition for use of private property as a normal way of life, and that allegations of crime are essentially challenges to such attempts at 'appropriation'. It follows that use of a substantial body of the kind of criminal law found in the United States signifies continued social recognition that a substantial portion of behaviour among the general populace is susceptible to being labelled criminal, indeed that far more behaviour has the injurious character of crime than that against which administrators apply the law. Even within existing law, Wallerstein and Wyle (1947) found it possible to get a random sample of New York State residents to accuse themselves of committing crimes at the rate of about one crime per two adults per year. Herein lie the seeds of findings that rates of crime tend to grow continually in the United States. But how inevitable is it that these seeds take root, sprout and continue through a growth cycle?

The seeds of the growth of crime get ample nurture from an outgrowth of widespread appropriative behaviour: a class hierarchy based on imputation of individual achievement. The capacity of a person to approximate private property is reinforced and recognised through attribution to persons of status or social position defined in relation to the appropriative capacities of others. An economically based social position is commonly called a 'class hierarchy'. As noted by Weber (1947:424—429), social positions may be conferred either through birthright or through acquisition of property. Development of social positions of the latter type is characteristic of societies dominated by appropriative behaviour, and forms the kind of class hierarchy prominent in the United States.

A salient class hierarchy makes the status identification (described in chapter 4) characteristic of American administrators feasible. Without a salient class hierarchy, application of the law against persons would become more perilous than it now is in the United States, for the administrator would be put in far greater jeopardy of having an attempted application of the law turned against him or her. A sense that lower-class people can be identified with some popular consensus lends security to use of the law as a weapon against the interests of members of that class. By thus facilitating the application of the law, a salient class hierarchy in turn facilitates the growth of officially recognised crime.

A salient class hierarchy facilitates the growth of crime in another way, too. Recall from Part I of this book that the administrator must base decisions as to how to apply the law on indeterminate evidence of whether a person has 'really' committed a crime. Furthermore, even if the administrator decides that that particular person has 'really' committed a crime, the law generally leaves wide latitude to decide how severe a sanction should be imposed as a consequence. In a moral sense, is a crime to be regarded as a unique and uncharacteristic act of a person who generally has earned high community regard, or is the crime evidence of a person's generally low character? In a predictive sense, is commission of a crime evidence that special precautions should be taken to protect the community from the offender in the future, or is the risk worth taking that the offender will be more of a help than a bother to others if left at liberty? To make matters harder for the administrator, research (like that by Wenk and Emrich, 1972) tends to indicate that predictions that particular persons will commit crimes in the future are apt to prove wrong more often than not. Criteria for application of the law, like the stereotypes by which police fulfil prophecies (described in chapter 4), are indispensable to anything but intolerably capricious decision-making. A salient class hierarchy has consistently provided a guide to selection of such criteria. Without a class hierarchy to guide decision-making, official finding of crime in the United States would be practically without foundation.

Some of the criteria, all class-related, used by American administrators to identify criminals have been described in chapter 4 as stereotypes used by police. As far as can be seen, no administrative criterion for identifying criminals has been developed by American administrators which has not been echoed in social science literature on crime causation. The criteria are well articulated in the literature. A survey of a representative sample of the crime causation theories reveals how fundamental salient class distinctions are to locating criminals. For instance, there are theoretical explanations of crime as a predominantly male phenomenon (such as that of Miller, 1958), which support the marked tendency of administrators of the criminal law to focus their search for criminals among men (see Pollak, 1950) and find them in that group. What sustains Miller's theory? His discovery that gang violence in his sample could largely be traced to boys from the lower-class homes that were especially apt to be fatherless. From this base, he reasons that the violence was an attempt to establish a masculine identity not provided by a father figure in the home.

To the degree that class distinctions were attenuated, Miller's identification of a homogeneous group as a data base for location of a factor associated with delinquency (here treated as a category of crime as a social problem) would be rendered increasingly problematic. In turn, support for one guideline to locating delinquency (as a category of criminals) would become increasingly tenuous.

The range of crime causation theories is broad. To begin with, there is a group of theories that traces crime to a failure of personal adjustment on the part of the criminal. Such failure may be traced to any one or more of a number of factors. One of the factors claimed to cause criminal behaviour has been biological deficiency, such as by Hooton, who claimed that for biologically defective offenders 'it is impossible to improve and correct environment to a point at which these flawed and degenerate human beings will be able to succeed in honest social competition' (1939:388). Regardless of the variety of biological explanation, the resultant failure of social adjustment would be held to be indicated not only by the commission of crimes but by economic failure as well. The connection between poverty and criminality is at the root of practically all crime causation theories, in recognition of the high probability of those labelled criminal coming from the lower or lower middle class. If the biological theorists found that officially labelled criminals had a significant chance of rising high in the economic hierarchy, they could be expected to find their claims of social maladjustment untenable.

Another group of theories traces criminal behaviour to interrupted psychological development. Aichhorn's (1955) theory falls into this category. According to Aichhorn, the true psychological criminal does not remain officially hidden; instead, he arranges his or her own detection in order to assuage his or her own guilt. The commission of crime itself is a form of self-punishment which these theorists would be hard put to it to reconcile with economic success. Here too, theories of crime causation are made tenable by the coincidence of officially detected criminality and poverty. In the less classically psychoanalytic but still psychological theories of crime (or delinquency) causation, such as that by Healy and Bronner (1936), poverty itself is seen as a source of emotional disturbance producing offence behaviour.

This points to the group of theories that looks directly to social forces as sources of criminal acts. Based on Sutherland's idea that criminal behaviour is learned from definitions favourable to commission of crime through interaction with others (see Sutherland and Cressey, 1970), a series of theories has focused on how the condition of enforced poverty fosters the development and institutionalisation of such favourable definitions. Aspects of the condition of enforced poverty leading to definitions favouring criminality, it has been argued, include insufficient legitimate means to attain the dominant societal goal of economic success (see, e.g., Merton, 1957:131–194, on 'anomie', followed by Cloward and Ohlin, 1960), poor educational opportunities and support (see, e.g., Cohen, 1955), a foreign cultural background (see, e.g., Sellin, 1938) and an inadequate family situation (see, e.g., Glueck and Glueck, 1951). A line of thinking known as 'the Chicago school' or 'the ecological school' (traceable to the work of Thrasher, 1963, and Shaw and McKay, 1972) finds that criminality stems from physical conditions associated with living in poverty. 'The subculture of violence' has been held to arise out of poverty (Wolfgang and Ferracuti, 1967:298).

In the tradition of Tannenbaum (1938) and Lemert (1951), responsibility for recurrent criminality in individuals has been placed on the purported disabling effects of official labelling of the criminal offender. What is held to make such widespread labelling possible? The

109

easy identification by administrators of relatively powerless poor persons who have difficulty in challenging the labels given them. Without a lower class, widespread labelling would be apt to become politically unfeasible, and labelling theorists would be hard pressed for a basis to predict criminal recidivism.

If a lower-class position can be taken as evidence corroborating criminality, a higher-class position can be inferred as likely evidence of success in unscrupulous behaviour that should be especially severely treated as crime. Such thinking has its origins in the work of Karl Marx. On the one hand, official labelling of criminals is seen as a device to keep the poor in their place, and to consolidate the positions of those in higher classes. Crimes are believed to be identified and punished by the state in order to maintain the class order. On the other hand, the 'real' criminals, those in the higher classes, commit their predatory offences to accumulate more capital (see, e.g., Quinney, 1974). From the point of view of this set of theorists, if class distinctions become attenuated, it can only be because the quest for accumulation of capital has lost its social power. Hence, the basis held to cause the commission of 'real' crime and the false labelling of other crime would be undermined, and these phenomena would become relics of the past.

From all these different perspectives, regardless of which is accepted among administrators or those in the populace, isolation of criminals is hard to support without reference to a salient class hierarchy. It would seem to follow that the probability of application of the law against crime in a populace would decrease significantly with an attenuation of the salience of class distinctions.

*Cognitive Link between American Law and Crime*

As a concomitant of the right of mobility built into the substance of American formal written law, the dominant American ideology requires that class position be traceable to personal accomplishment — that the position of each person be traceable to achievement in an openly competitive market. Regardless of how people actually gain class position, class position is generally politically defensible only upon a showing that individuals characteristically earn their positions through their own efforts or lack thereof. In an admittedly feudal society, the

110

displaced poor might even be killed on sight as 'outlaws' — those who had no place in the ascriptive social order. In the United States, the labelling of criminality has been facilitated by making criminality an earned status *within* the social order. If an association between poverty and criminality is to be defended, it is because a similar inadequacy leads to both, not because denial of social and economic support itself implies outlawry. To those to whom the poor are seen as victims of a criminal justice system, the poor are victims of the personal wrong-doings of those higher in the class system, not of the workings of a system in which people are born into roles beyond personal control. Similarly, those Americans who do not blame the poor for their economic status tend to blame individuals of a higher class for enforcing the poverty of others. To some American critics, people at the bottom of the class hierarchy need the greatest assistance from the law to compete on a more nearly equal basis with those above them, but the cultural premise of the necessity of interpersonal competition for property and power remains firmly fixed in the critics' thinking. General social acceptance of appropriation as a typical way of life is a necessary condition for social importance to be given to our class hierarchy. If Americans who regarded the acquisition of private property to the denial of others' access a foolish and trivial waste of time were not also typically viewed by other Americans (forming a majority) as strange or crazy, there would be practically no political foundation for giving social significance to a class hierarchy.

By extension, if the populace and the administrators of the criminal law give substantial support to the finding and labelling of criminals, the assumption must be widely held that individual competition for guarantees of future access to economic resources is a typical and legitimate way of life. By extension, such reliance reinforces social support (a) for the maintenance of a salient class hierarchy, and thereby (b) for the finding and labelling of criminals.

In particular, two elements of the American criminal law concept of responsibility combine to ratify popular acceptance of a class hierarchy and its underlying ethic of individualism. To be responsible before the law, a person must be found to have acted as a cause-in-fact of a proscribed presumably social injury, and the person must be inferred to have made an individual decision to commit the act. In legal jargon, the person must have committed an *actus reus* (a 'wrongful act') with *mens rea* (a 'guilty mind').

111

On the one hand, this means that the person must be inferred reasonably to have been able to anticipate that the injury would not have resulted 'but for' his or her act. Hence, a defendant has been held not guilty of manslaughter, whose beating only speeded the death of a victim who apparently would have died of disease even without the beating (Virginia Supreme Court, 1857). Another defendant was held not guilty of murder who shot a victim, after which the victim died not of the wound but of scarlet fever communicated by an attending physician (Kentucky Court of Appeals, 1880). The line is often difficult and ambiguous to draw as to where the causal nexus is sufficiently close to warrant conviction of a crime, but the point of importance here is that administrators of the law are literally called upon by the terms to apply the law only against those persons whose behaviour is a direct source of injury to others.

To be convicted in an American court, a person must be inferred to have chosen by exercise of free will to have committed the *actus reus*. There is ambiguity in establishing an operational definition of this requirement for application of the criminal law against a person, too. Children under the age of seven are generally presumed to be incapable of such choice. Other tests used have included whether the accused 'had or had not the use of his understanding, so as to know that he was doing a wrong or wicked act' (House of Lords, 1843), whether the act resulted from an 'uncontrollable' or 'irresistible impulse' (see Mississippi Supreme Court, 1879), whether the person 'lacked substantial capacity to know or appreciate the wrong or harm he has done' (see New York Penal Law, 1967), whether the act was the 'product of a mental disease or defect' (see District of Columbia Court of Appeals, 1954), whether the person was awake when committing the act (see Kentucky Court of Appeals, 1879).

In sum, the question addressed by the law of criminal responsibility is whether the person has acted so as to have earned criminal status as an individual achievement. Just as the class hierarchy is built on the foundation of individuals being considered to have earned their positions in it, the application of the criminal law against persons is built on the foundation of the persons' having earned offender status. Correlatively, the message communicated by the concept of criminal responsibility is that no other collectively imposed obligation stands in the way of individualism. By circumscribing the substantive requirements for attachment of social responsibility, and by building procedural safeguards against criminal conviction that make the probability of receiving criminal sanctions minimal for most among the populace, formal support is lent to a popular notion that obligations to interpersonal cooperation are few and far between. The ethic supporting the salience of the class hierarchy and the ethic represented to the populace and administrators of the criminal law by the concept of criminal responsibility are one and the same. Whether one goes to prison or becomes wealthy is a matter of individual responsibility; dependence on others for support is no defence to a charge of crime and no right or socially prominent guarantee. The law thus encourages the kind of injurious behaviour it is formally supposed to restrict.


## Conclusion

We have now seen an inseparable chain of institutions which together receive strong popular support in the American cultural context: a compendious body of written criminal law which prescribes negative sanctions for people found individually responsible for causing social injury, reward for individual accomplishment, a lack of commitment to maintenance of particular interpersonal relationships, interpersonal competition and distrust, high rates of legally protected social mobility, private property, routine appropriation of resources to others' disadvantage, widespread challenge to appropriation, routine administration of the criminal law, considerable administrative discretion to apply the criminal law on principles independent of the terms of the law themselves, socio-economic bias in the application of the law, administrative attempts at deception to try to preserve the appearance of doing justice, and a continued growth in official rates of crime.

Sufficient popular support for dramatic change in any one of these institutions would *require* sufficient popular support for changes in the others. Conversely (for the symbiotic relationship among the institutions represents a kind of equation), sufficient popular support for a dramatic change in any one of these institutions would *imply* sufficient popular support for changes in the others. Not only is this symbiosis consistent with the empirical data already adduced, but to suggest a failure of symbiosis so widespread that the symbiosis would not be reflected in the mainstream of popular opinion is to suggest a societal

113

failure of cognitive consistency of practically unimaginable proportions. Hence, if a way is to be found to change one of the institutions dramatically throughout American society, the way must also be a path to change in the other institutions as well. This appears to be a precondition to extended change in any and all of the institutions.

A problem of major proportion is posed for Americans who want to plan seriously for reductions in societal crime rates. To accomplish this end, are they prepared to sacrifice existing opportunities to move through the social system? Are they prepared to let more people go legally unpunished for crime? Are those in relatively advantageous economic positions prepared to give at least part of the advantage away? A sustained drop in crime rates will come only at a variety of personal costs. Is the overall expenditure worthwhile? It is beyond the scope of this book to attempt to answer such a complex and value-laden question. All that is suggested is a recognition that a personal choice to support any one of these institutions is of necessity a choice to support the others also.

Without advocating change in the chain of institutions, some ideas can be developed to stimulate thinking about how the change might be accomplished if it were to be pursued. Americans have become so accustomed to relying on law to attempt social control that law readily comes to mind as an instrument of change. Since it appears that growth of crime rates is linked to a particular form of law, rather than to law *per se*, new forms of law could conceivably help to effect widespread changes in American patterns of behaviour. As a prelude to careful consideration of how a change in the chain of institutions might practically be achieved, some tentative legislative proposals are set forth in the following two chapters.

REFERENCES

Aichhorn, August. 1955. *Wayward Youth*. New York: Meridian Books.

Cloward, Richard A., and Lloyd A. Ohlin. 1960. *Delinquency and Opportunity: A Theory of Delinquent Gangs*. New York: Free Press.

Cohen, Albert K. 1955. *Delinquent Boys: The Culture of the Gang*. New York: Free Press.

District of Columbia Court of Appeals. 1954. *Durham v. United States*. 214 F.2d 862.

Glueck, Sheldon, and Eleanor Glueck. 1951. *Unraveling Juvenile Delinquency*. Cambridge, Mass.: Harvard University Press.

Healy, William, and Augusta F. Bronner. 1936. *New Light on Delinquency and its Treatment*. New Haven: Yale University Press.

Hooton, Ernest A. 1939. *Crime and the Man*. Cambridge, Mass.: Harvard University Press.

House of Lords. 1843. *M'Naghten's Case*, 10 Cl. and F. 200, 8 Eng. Reprint 718.

Kentucky Court of Appeals. 1879. *Fain v. Commonwealth*. 78 Ky. 183.

Kentucky Court of Appeals. 1880. *Bush v. Commonwealth*. 78 Ky. 268.

Lemert, Edwin M. 1951. *Social Pathology*. New York: McGraw-Hill Book Company.

Merton, Robert K. 1957. *Social Theory and Social Structure*. New York: Free Press (rev. edn).

Miller, Walter B. 1958. 'Lower class culture as a generating milieu of gang delinquency'. *Journal of Social Issues*, 14 (November):5–19.

Mississippi Supreme Court. 1879. *Cunningham v. State*. 56 Miss. 269.

New York Penal Law. 1967. 'Mental disease or defect'. Sec. 30.05.

Pollak, Otto. 1950. *The Criminality of Women*. Philadelphia: University of Pennsylvania Press.

Quinney, Richard. 1974. *Critique of Legal Order: Crime Control in Capitalist Society*. Boston: Little, Brown and Company.

Sellin, Thorsten. 1938. *Culture Conflict and Crime*. New York: Social Science Research Council.

Shaw, Clifford, R., and Henry D. McKay. 1972. *Juvenile Delinquency and Urban Areas*. Chicago: University of Chicago Press (rev. edn).

Sutherland, Edwin H., and Donald R. Cressey. 1970. *Principles of Criminology*. Philadelphia: J. B. Lippincott and Company (8th ed).

Tannenbaum, Frank. 1938. *Crime and the Community*. Boston: Ginn and Company.

Thrasher, Frederic M. (abridged edition, James F. Short Jr., ed). 1963. *Gang: A Study of One Thousand Three Hundred Thirteen Gangs in Chicago*. Chicago: University of Chicago Press.

United States Court of Appeals for the District of Columbia. 1954. *Durham v. United States*. 214 F.2d 862.

Virginia Supreme Court. 1857. *Livingston v. Commonwealth*. 14 Gratt. (55 Va.) 592.

Wallerstein, James S., and Clement J. Wyle. 1947. 'Our law-abiding law-breakers'. *Probation*, 25 (March–April):105–112.

Weber, Max (A. M. Henderson and Talcott Parsons, trans.; Talcott Parsons, ed.). 1947. *Max Weber: The Theory of Social and Economic Organization*. New York: Free Press.

Wenk, Ernst A., and Robert L. Emrich. 1972. 'Assaultive Youth'. *Journal of Research on Crime and Delinquency*, 9 (July):179–196.

Wolfgang, Marvin E., and Franco Ferracuti. 1967. *The Subculture of Violence: Towards an Integrated Theory in Criminology*. London: Tavistock Publications.

# PART III

# Ideas for Legislating Crime Control in the United States

# 8. LEGISLATION OF POSITIVE INCENTIVES IN THE UNITED STATES

*Introduction*

Positive incentives have rarely been legislated for crime control in the United States, but they deserve serious consideration. Generically, legislation of positive incentives has one major advantage over legislation of negative incentives, although there does not currently appear to be any inherent difference in the effects of administration of positive and negative incentives (which may also be called 'stimuli', 'sanctions', or 'reinforcers'):

> The research and theories on punishment, escape, and avoidance are all compatible with the following hypothesis: aversive stimuli function in the same manner as do positive reinforcers. Rewards and punishments are events that are identical but opposite in sign in their effect on behavior. No separate laws need to be constructed to understand the effects of aversive stimuli. Although this conclusion is simple and consistent with extant data, it is only very recently that it has begun to gain acceptance. (Fantino, 1973:275)

The difference arises instead out of one of the conditions of effective use of incentives: that, in operant conditioning, the incentive must be applied soon after (and only after) the behaviour that is to be modified or strengthened. In the laboratory, one can easily monitor behaviour and respond appropriately with administration of rewards and aversive stimuli. Such is not the case outside the laboratory in a large, open and complex social system.

More often than not, when the prospect of an official negative sanction threatens an actor at large in a social system, the actor will

119

quite simply and naturally seek to conceal either his or her identity or the occurrence of sanctionable behaviour or both. When, for instance, the national clearance rate by arrest of officially known burglaries is approximately 10 per cent, criminal punishment of burglars can theoretically have only limited effectiveness.

On the other hand, when the availability of an official positive incentive is made known to an actor in a social system, the actor can be expected to make his or her identity and rewardable behaviour readily known, so that the incentive can be administered. Of course, the effectiveness of the positive incentive would in theory be substantially reduced if the administrator delayed application for long out of fear of responding to a false claim. But this problem can be overcome, as it generally has been in American administrative response to tax returns even at a national level.

Hence, the use of positive incentives in the criminal justice system can be expected to affect the behaviour of the populace far more dramatically than the use of negative incentives. Moreover, the administrator of the criminal law is relieved of responsibility for making socially biased searches for places to apply the law. And challenges to appropriation and charges of discrimination more readily arise from perceived loss than from perceived gain. Even from the Marxist perspective in criminology, outrage over the oppression of the working poor seems to outweigh anger over the benefits (including a kind of alienative slavery) seen to accrue to the rich capitalists. Granted, it does seem important to structure incentives so that their benefits are relatively equally available to those throughout the class hierarchy, but it is far easier to plan a relatively equal distribution of benefits when the subjects of the incentives can be expected to cooperate in their identification rather than to try to avoid detection.

Two sets of incentives are proposed here. One set is more directly addressed to decreasing use of the kind of criminal law that supports the growth of crime rates, while the other set is more directly addressed to attenuating the class hierarchy that also supports such growth.


*Proposed Legislation*


A.    *It is proposed that the law provide that government subsidies be*

120

*paid to any administrator of the criminal law, except a prosecutor or judge, or a court services officer preparing pre-sentence reports, for periodic decreases in the number of official reports on cases which he or she officially makes.*

In part, such a programme has already been implemented in Orange County, California, where patrolmen get increases in pay for decreases in the rates at which they officially report rapes, robberies, car thefts and burglaries. In the first sixteen months of this programme, the rate of report of these offences in the area declined by 19 per cent, though reported rates of unsubsidised offences increased (Greiner, 1974; Holsendolph, 1974). Also, subsidies have proved effective in diverting people to probation from commitment to state institutions throughout California (see Saleeby, 1971), though the proposal made here would divert people even from probation.

Prosecutors, judges and court services officers preparing pre-sentence reports are excepted from the proposal for two reasons. First, they are expected to oppose the proposal strongly, out of deference to the manifest American ethic of independence of the decision-making of the courts from considerations other than the merits of the cases they consider. Even though these administrators of the courts operate under the same constraints as others, the sanctity of unfettered discretion of those in the courts is strongly protected by appellate judges, who would be more likely to hold application of the proposal to these administrators than to others to be an unlawful interference with due process in violation of the Fifth and Fourteenth Amendments of the United States Constitution. In other words, application of the proposal to these administrators of the courts would be less politically feasible than would application of the proposal to other administrators.

Second, the effect of the application of the proposal on administrators of the courts would probably be the opposite of that desired. The most obvious way for them to try to cut down their number of official reports would be to give longer sentences to defendants, with the thought that this would eventually cut down on the number of recidivist cases they were given to handle. The effect would be positively rather than negatively to reinforce the labelling of persons as criminals.

For other administrators, however, an effect of adoption of the proposal would be to reward curtailment of the labelling of criminals. By being encouraged to file fewer offence reports, arrest reports and

121

incident reports or memoranda, the police would be expected to find fewer crimes and criminals. Court clerks would be expected to discourage citizens from filing criminal complaints. The rate of institution of probation and parole revocation proceedings should drop off. Parole boards would be induced to grant earlier paroles, so that fewer hearings would be recorded for each inmate. Correctional staffs would be discouraged from instituting formal disciplinary proceedings in jails and prisons. On the whole, the effect of the adoption of the proposal should be to displace formal intervention in cases of social conflict by greater reliance on informal handling of interpersonal disputes.

This proposal is not to be confused with straightforward abolition of formal criminal justice institutions. Thus, for instance, it is inappropriate to project that the expected social response to adoption of this proposal concerning the police would be like the social response to a police labour strike (as has Hutchins, 1973:1). In times of social crisis, when danger to life and limb were in immediate peril with private resolution not in sight, the police would still be available to intervene. It might make an officer a little more reluctant to arrest a husband in a family shouting match simply because the husband called the officer a not-so-nice name, but not to disarm a drunken husband brandishing a gun and to give the husband a little time to sober up in confinement. A parole officer would probably still take official action against his parolee if he heard the parolee were out to shoot someone, but the parole officer might show greater reluctance to revoke the parole of a man for getting married without permission.

There is no reason, in other words, to believe that adoption of the proposal would lead administrators to abandon all responsibility for intervention in dangerous situations. But it could be expected to restrain administrators from intervention in the plethora of trivial cases in which the social danger presented is apparently neither great nor imminent. For instance, adoption of the proposal might lead to a substantial reduction in arrests for vagrancy and disorderly conduct, which together persist in accounting for more than 10 per cent of arrests made nationwide in the United States. By contrast, the likelihood that adoption would affect the rate of arrests for criminal homicide (less than one arrest in 400 nationwide) would be minimal (see Federal Bureau of Investigation, annual).

The proposal is designed to reduce the rate of socio-economically discriminatory application of the criminal law, and to promote the expectation among the American general populace that interpersonal disputes would more commonly need to be resolved through private cooperation. If greater reliance on private relationships (rather than on the state) were engendered for dealing with personal problems, development and maintenance of community ties might be expected to gain importance among the populace, leading to declines in rates of social mobility.

Political support for the proposal could be promoted by arguing that its implementation would cut down on state expenditure (and hence, perhaps, on taxes). In property crimes especially, but also in most crimes against the person, the damage caused by an officially labelled crime seldom approaches the cost of institutionalising the offender (now averaging around $15,000 per person per year in correctional costs alone in the United States). No less an economically concerned group than the national Chamber of Commerce has recognised the power of the financial argument in crime control, leading it to advocate community treatment for most persons now sent to jail or prison. However, many private persons might still resist the proposal out of fear that they would be incapable of managing interpersonal conflicts without assistance. Provision of some new form of dispute resolution assistance might be needed to control such fear. The second proposal is directed to this problem.

B. *It is proposed that part of the money saved by adoption of the first proposal be devoted to creation and maintenance of social support service agencies that (a) are prohibited from setting any conditions on initiation or continuation of client contact, (b) are prohibited from keeping files containing any information that is not already in the public domain, (c) cannot act as parties to any formal legal action, and (d) can take any action on a case only in the client's physical presence.*

It is to be expected that many private persons, given added responsibility for management of community problems, would need emotional support, common-sense advice based on prior experience, and information about available community resources, to facilitate attempts to resolve interpersonal conflicts. Such support, advice and information would often be found lacking among a relatively inexperienced general populace. If properly structured, public social support services could give valuable assistance to many people in real need, thereby facilitating social movement away from reliance on application of criminal law and toward private dispute settlement.

If social support services are on the one hand to reinforce positively people's sense that they can privately resolve conflicts, and on the other hand to reinforce negatively a reliance on formal written law, certain safeguards need to be built into the service structure. For one thing, the client needs to be given a sense that he or she has responsibility for the ultimate determination of what is to be done about his or her problem, and about what constitutes the problem itself. This requires that the service agency should not set the terms of what constitute valid problems, or of when the problems have been dealt with as best they can be. This is the reason for the prohibition of any conditions being set by the agency for initiating or continuing client contact.

The threat posed by files of information on people has become a major social issue in common-law countries. (For a good recent study of the issue, see Rule, 1974.) The threat does not reside in the existence *per se* of information about people. Information about people can be a tool needed to help them as well as to hurt them. The problems of the holding of information arise from (a) the creation of new categories into which to place people based on the information, and (b) limitations placed on access of certain people to the information (especially on access by the person the information concerns directly). Categorisation of the person tends to rigidify the response to the person and to detract from the ability of the person to manage the situation and adapt it to his or her needs. Information file categories about people, especially in social services, tend to be derogatory and demeaning — to lead to paternalistic agency response at best and antagonistic or suspicious response at worst. Files containing such information about clients of a social service could be expected more to frustrate than to assist their bids for assistance.

Limitations on access to such information pose a similar and yet distinct problem. When derogatory information about the client is gathered, the natural reaction is to keep the information from the client in order not to compromise the sources of information. On the one hand, this presents a barrier to the client's communication with agency staff, for he or she cannot be clear on the basis for response to him or her. On the other hand, the client can be confronted with the attitude that the staff member knows more about the client than does the client himself or herself. This hardly lends itself to positive reinforcement of the client's feeling of being able to handle responsibility for management of his or her own interpersonal problems. By restricting files to information that is already in the public domain, there is no ground for failure to share the contents of the file with the client, and the agency staff are deterred from formalising their own categorisations of clients. The client's self-reliance is therefore apt to receive more positive reinforcement than would otherwise be the case. Keeping confidential information out of files altogether also obviates the kind of antagonism generated between administrators and clients even over legally protected client access to and consent to disposition of, file information, such as is provided to students and parents in a recently enacted American law (United States Public Law, 1974).

Recall that a major deleterious effect of popular reliance on American criminal law — an effect these proposals are designed to attenuate — is that people learn to rely increasingly on administrators to take over their problems for them. This would be anticipated to be the direct effect of permitting social services to become parties to legal actions, criminal or civil, on their clients' behalf. Hence, social services would be prohibited from so acting under this proposal.

For this same reason, it would be undesirable for a client to have any sense that his or her case had been 'turned over' to the social service agency. It is therefore necessary to stress the direct involvement of the client in all phases of dealing with his or her problem. This is the reason for the requirement of the client's physical presence when any action is taken on his or her case.

Given such a structure, social services might stand a reasonable chance of helping people to rely less on law and more on their own continued involvement in managing interpersonal problems. Such services could also help those among the populace to resolve interpersonal conflicts without so readily resorting to social mobility, and to build confidence in ability to achieve interpersonal cooperation.

C.  *It is proposed that the law provide that:*

*1. Subsidy be given the American employer for* (a) *each additional full-time employee employed during the employer's tax year, the number of additional full-time employees employed being equal to the excess of the average number for the current tax year over that for the previous tax year of those employed each regular working day for at least six hours and paid at least the Federal minimum wage,*

125

*PROVIDED that* (b) *the employer will be eligible for the subsidy only if the percentage of increase in the average daily wage (including value of fringe benefits) of the lowest paid full-time employee from the previous tax year to the current tax year is greater than the percentage of increase in the national consumer price index for the same period.*

*2. Taxes will be levied against the employer* (a) *for reduction in the number of full-time employees employed during the tax year, and* (b) *for the extent to which the percentage of increase in the national consumer price index exceeds the percentage of change in the average daily wage (including value of fringe benefits) of the lowest paid full-time employee from the prior tax year to the current tax year.*

*3. In computing the subsidy and taxes, an employer acquiring an existing business will be required to account for the numbers and wages of employees in that business prior to acquisition. The optimal amounts of the subsidy and taxes remain to be determined.*

The language of the proposal may look complicated (like many of the provisions of the United States Internal Revenue Code), but the terms of the proposal are relatively simple. In essence, each employer would be rewarded by the law for hiring more people and keeping the compensation of the lowest paid employee ahead of the pace of inflation, or be penalised for failing to do so. Here, positive and negative incentives are combined, but the proposal is set forth in this chapter because it is designed to elicit rewarding behaviour. The taxes are included to make it more attractive for employers to try to earn the subsidy than to fail to make the effort out of calculation that the chances of qualifying for the subsidy are not worth the attempt.

The proposal is designed primarily to decrease unemployment and to decrease the employment income disparity between lower- and higher-paid employees, to help accomplish an attenuation of class distinctions in our society. To minimise the amount of tax liability and to increase the probability of receiving a subsidy instead, the employer would be directed to concentrate on making room for steadily more employees and on increasing the compensation of workers at the bottom of the income ladder as steadily and rapidly as possible.

Because the number of employees would be calculated on a daily and then annual basis, the employer could not adjust for hiring at some times by firing at others. When more work was to be done, the incentive would be offered for hiring more full-time employees rather than for paying existing employees for more overtime. Including only those employees working at least a six-hour day in the subsidy computation would discourage individually small compensation to merely part-time employees.

Nor could the employer compensate for increased hiring by lowering wages at the bottom of the pay scale, for to do so would increase the employer's tax burden. As is true with hiring and firing, increased wages at one point in time could not be offset by decreased wages at another. Fringe benefits could not be reduced to offset increased wages, for fringe benefits would be included in the computations.

The national consumer price index has been chosen as a measure of inflation rather than each employer's prices because price increases could be too easily camouflaged from official view. Higher prices could be attached to what was advertised as a new product, or if average prices for all the employer's products were used for computation, price levels could be maintained while less costly products were more heavily produced. Change in the consumer price index is also thought to be the measure of inflation most directly related to change in the economic position of the lower-paid employees.

Even though the increase in the consumer price index could not precisely be known until the tax year had passed, the current consumer price index rather than past figures alone would have to figure in the computation if the rate of inflation were not to be induced to increase at ever higher rates from year to year. However, because of possible miscalculation and because any one employer might raise prices out of a sense that its (or his or her) price policy alone would not determine the consumer price index, use of the current consumer price index itself would introduce a risk of inflation.

Nevertheless, the problem of inflation should not be severe for a number of reasons. First, the major corporations, those in a position to contribute more to inflation, should correspondingly be expected to exercise the greatest price restraint for fear of contributing directly to their own tax burdens. Second, to the extent that the rate of increase in the consumer price index exceeded wage increases for the lowest-paid employees, an increasing tax burden would remove more money from circulation in the economy, exerting a pressure against inflation. Third, a greater number of better paid employees should produce more supply for the enlarged consumer market they represent, to offer the producer more income to offset increased employment expenses even at steady prices. Fourth, even if technological and logistical improvements could

127

not keep pace with increasing marginal costs of production resulting from increased hiring and wages, the more efficient producers should be able to use the subsidy to offset those costs.

As with any major shift in economic policy, there is a risk that employers with marginal profits would go out of business, contributing to unemployment. One must in part count on the determination of employers to go to new lengths to remain in business. In cases where marginally increasing labour costs could not be offset by the introduction of technological logistic innovation, the rate of increase in compensation to employees other than those lowest paid and/or the employer's profits themselves would probably be curtailed.

Where increased costs were taken out of employee compensation, white-collar employees would probably be the group hardest hit. With labour unions as strong as they are, employers could scarcely afford blatant discrimination against blue-collar workers. Should increases in compensation of white-collar employees (who could more easily than others afford to save or invest more substantial parts of their income) be curtailed, a greater incentive would be offered to white-collar workers to generate income from saving and investment, which in turn would help to provide capital to support needed increases in employment.

To the extent that adoption of the proposal accomplished its desired end, the cost of administering the government would be reduced. Increased employment would lower the welfare burden, and a decreasing salience of class distinctions would be expected to contribute to a reduction of the burden of maintaining the criminal justice system. The proposal could be administered by the United States Internal Revenue Service without much additional cost. These savings to government could be used to finance the subsidy. In an initial period of stimulation of private employment, it would also be expected that employers would hire those who had already been working for the government. Therefore, there might be a period in which increasing private employment did not affect the overall rate of unemployment, but such circumstances should be temporary.

There are two major implicit elements of the proposal which are deemed necessary to a genuine attenuation of the salience of class distinctions in the American social system. One element is that increases in the personal income of those at the bottom of the economic order are given in exchange for labour, while government

128

benefits are conferred on those higher in the economic order. One primary means of stigmatising the poor in our society is to make them recipients of 'welfare' payments with the implicit understanding that, unlike others, these recipients are incapable of earning their own support. It is preferable, therefore, to have the employers suffer whatever stigma accompanies receipt of government subsidy, that burdens of class be more equally distributed. If the class identity of the poor is to lose salience, it is necessary that the rate at which they receive income as a product of employment in private enterprise should increase. If the payment of government benefits is not to be a means of reinforcing the social salience of a person's being poor, the benefits must go to those whose *earning* of income in exchange for labour is already generally taken for granted. Improvements in the economic position of the poor must be typically attributed to contributions the poor make to the productive order rather than being viewed as necessary burdens on that order. Hence, increasing income of the poor under this proposal is considered preferable to increasing it in the form of welfare or negative income tax payments.

The second element is for the law to represent the view that the economic interests of those high in the economic order are tied not to the maintenance of class positions but to their attenuation. Proposals can and have been made (such as the universal wage-rate subsidy, see Barth, 1972) by which wage increases would supposedly outpace inflation, but such proposals explicitly fail to provide for attenuation of class disparity. The law needs to suggest to employees that their personal benefit depends on giving steadily more income to those in the lower class than is supported by increased prices to lower-class consumers.

For some time now, it has been an economic truism that a choice had to be made between providing more people with sources of income and providing people with more spending power. This prophecy continues to fulfil itself. The problem of maintenance of class distinctions arises not so much from acceptance of this premise as from acceptance of the premise that those at the bottom of the economic order must gain least and suffer most as the trade-off is made: that those who lack employment must ever give disproportionate benefit to employers if the former are ultimately to be supported by employment at all. Here is another manifestation of a system of appropriation, the inevitable competition of interests between employers and those who need employment. This proposal is designed to help to convert those interests to cooperative ones. Such a transition requires that those who need to be employed do not have to suffer an economic loss in order that employers may make economic headway. Instead, if the salience of class distinctions is to be attenuated, the economic headway of the employers must be made to depend on relative advancement of the position of those in the lower class.

Were the proposal adopted so that employers could no longer benefit at the disproportionate expense of those further down the economic ladder, employers would be left with two choices. Either they could play the economic game of inter-class cooperation, or they could abandon (but hardly liquidate, if no one were willing to be an employer) their assets and refuse to be employers at all. If the latter course were followed, capital assets would pass to the state by escheat or by deed of gift. It is hard to visualise a significant number of employers abdicating private enterprise simply because others were beginning or threatening to move toward them in the class hierarchy.

Assuming, then, that private employers continued to stay in business, private enterprise would be confronted with meeting the incentives of a new kind of economic challenge: how can the technology and logistics of production be accommodated to consolidating or expanding profits without resort to higher prices and with the expansion of a better-paid labour force? American employers may not have had much experience in such enterprise, but application of the ingenuity that has led to unprecedented economic growth in American society in the past should be up to the challenge of making money without promoting inter-class competition.

If a proposal like this were to work as planned, class distinctions should become less salient in American society. Employer—employee competition would tend to be displaced by experience in cooperation for mutual gain. Increased employee satisfaction and job security should tend to reduce occupational mobility. Symbiotically, crime rates should tend to decline.


*Conclusion*

Proposals like those made here are likely to strike an American audience as being 'radical' and dangerous. But the proposals are of a kind that is benign in a way atypical for American approaches to social control, whether radical or conventional. They rest on a faith that people can be trusted to cooperate in interpersonal affairs, that law designed to control crime need not be directed exclusively against evil people who require incapacitation, treatment, punishment or liquidation. To be sure, Americans are not accustomed to thinking about legislating crime control in such a fashion. But neither are they accustomed to accomplishing reductions in rates of crime through the use of law.

Undoubtedly, these proposals will bear considerable refinement. As they are novel, so they are bound to be found primitive in the light of further thinking. If the proposals are implemented, their effects may attenuate over time. Perhaps the proposals are unworkable because the kind of faith that underlies them is in itself naïve and unwarranted in the American context. Perhaps the advantages Americans derive from such things as mobility and interpersonal competition outweigh the cost of a continued growth in rates of crime. The proposals do not resolve or even address such issues. At best, the proposals reveal some previously unconsidered implications of making crime prevention effective in the United States. For the time being, that is the most the proposals are intended to accomplish.

REFERENCES

Barth, Michael C. 1972. 'Universal wage-rate subsidy: benefits and effects', in United States Congress Joint Economic Committee, *The Economics of Federal Subsidy Programs: Part 4 – Higher Education and Manpower Subsidies*, pp. 497–540. Washington, DC: United States Government Printing Office (28 August).
Fantino, Edmund. 1973. 'Aversive control', in John A. Nevin (ed.), *The Study of Behavior: Learning Motivation, Emotion and Instinct*, pp. 239–275. Glenview, Illinois: Scott, Foresman and Company.
Federal Bureau of Investigation. Annual. *Uniform Crime Reports*. Washington, DC: United States Government Printing Office.
Greiner, John M. 1974. *Tying City Pay to Performance: Early Reports on Orange, California and Flint, Michigan*. Washington, DC: Labor Management Relations Service of the National League of Cities, National Association of Counties, United States Conference of Mayors.
Holsendolph, Ernest. 1974. 'Police wage rate goes up if crime goes down'. *New York Times* (10 November):77.

Hutchins, Robert M. 1973. 'Comment on "toward diversion from diversion from the criminal justice system" '. Santa Barbara: Center for the Study of Democratic Institutions (paper presented at Second Criminal Justice Conference, 7 November).

Rule, James B. 1974. *Private Lives and Public Surveillance: Social Control in the Computer Age*. New York: Schocken Books.

Saleeby, George. 1971. 'Five years of probation subsidy'. *California Youth Authority Quarterly*, 24 (Fall):3–12.

United States Public Law. 1974. *The Family Educational Rights and Privacy Act of 1974*. Public Law, 93–380.

## 9.  LEGISLATION OF NEGATIVE INCENTIVES
IN THE UNITED STATES

*Introduction*

This chapter does not represent a withdrawal from the position taken in
the last chapter — that incorporation of positive incentives into the
crime control legislation is preferable to the incorporation of negative
incentives. However, as a less preferred step in the direction of altering
the kind of popular reliance on formal written criminal law and of
loosening constraints on the administration of the law, some changes
might be made in the kind of negative incentives the law provides.

One such change might be to replace the current concept of criminal
responsibility with a concept analogous to the American tort law
concept of joint and several responsibility. Responsibility for wrongdoing would be attributed to the collectivities of individuals, such as
corporations and municipalities, while the burden of responsibility
would be placed on every individual in the collectivity by imposition of
a fine on him or her. In other words, if the collectivity were found
responsible for wrongdoing, every individual within that collectivity
would be conclusively presumed to share that responsibility.

On the one hand, this change would structure the criminal law to
respond to collective as against individual accomplishment. On the
other hand, the change would at least raise the level of competition in
which administrators were involved from the arena of conflict of
individual interests to that of conflict of group interests. Appropriation
would be more abstract and therefore perhaps not induce such heated
challenge through the law. But the change could unite groups in more
powerful challenges to administrative decision-making than would
otherwise be made. Thus, while incorporation of a new type of negative
incentive into the American criminal law might change the pattern of

133

popular reliance on the law, it is not so clear that it would loosen constraints on administrators. Hence, if problems of application of the criminal law are to be addressed, incorporation of positive incentives into the law seems to be a clear choice over incorporation of negative incentives in any form.

And so the focus in this chapter is on altering popular response to criminal law rather than on resolving problems of administration of the law. The only way in which the proposal made here might facilitate administration is by eliminating the administrative requirement of making determinations of criminal intent or *mens rea*. Under the proposal, inferences concerning states of mind would be irrelevant to determinations of whether group actions had caused legally proscribed social injury. For instance, if emissions from a factory had polluted the air at proscribed levels, there would be no need to determine, who, if anyone, had intended the emissions, or whether the emissions were made by freewill choice. As is now the case in enforcement of environmental protection standards, proof of emissions would be sufficient to attach liability. As is *not* now the case, every employee of the factory and everyone owning interest in the factory would automatically be held individually liable for a violation of the criminal law.

While defendants under the provisions here proposed might include such collectivities as municipalities, the proposal will be developed with reference only to corporations. Corporations provide the best case in point because so much thought has already been given to how criminal liability might best be attached to collective wrongdoing there.

*Prior Experience with Problems of Imputing Responsibility for Corporate Crime*

Two basic approaches have been taken to imputing legal responsibility for corporate crime. One approach has been to try to find the particular corporate employees responsible for the criminal activity. The other approach has been to fine the corporation itself for crime committed on its behalf.

The first approach is illustrated by the prosecution and conviction of corporate executives in the electric company conspiracy cases discussed

134

in chapter 2 (see Geis, 1968, and Smith, 1961, for accounts of these cases). Here a number of executives were convicted of having engaged in a conspiracy to fix bids for the sale of heavy electrical equipment, including switchgear. Seven of the defendants received jail sentences of thirty days apiece. These defendants included vice-presidents, division heads and a sales manager.

There is no reason to question the deterrent effect of the sentences on the defendants themselves. While detailed evidence of the business practices of these defendants subsequent to release is not available, a plausible claim has been made that the effect on such 'respectable' defendants of receiving and serving a jail sentence was dramatic. As Cameron (1964) found in the case of 'naïve' shoplifters, people who have been cloaked in the respectability of unblemished membership in a middle or higher class prior to a criminal conviction are especially unlikely to be found to be recidivists, at least for the same offence. In part, this phenomenon seems to be attributable to the great psychological stake such people have in re-establishing their 'respectability'.

Thus the major problem of this approach to imputing responsibility for corporate crime does not appear to be the special deterrence of individual corporate defendants, but a failure to affect larger forces contributing to the commission of corporate crime. In the electric company cases, the defendants from General Electric were especially quick to point out that they had acted to meet the demands of loyal service to their employer. It may well be true that had any of the defendants in General Electric refused to participate in the price-fixing scheme, he would have been replaced by someone with sufficient corporate loyalty and ambition to do the job instead.

This sense of the expendability of any individual employee and of the inevitability of the ultimate commission of illicit corporate practices has been corroborated in other cases. Vandivier (1972) has reported on his experience as a testing engineer of involvement in the falsification of a qualification report for a brake for an Air Force jet. The brake consistently failed the qualification tests. When Vandivier refused to sign the falsified report that the brake met qualification standards, the report was sent on without his signature. When he reported the fraud to the Federal Bureau of Investigation, he was summarily fired. After repeated failures of the brake on the jets, the company manufacturing the brake substituted new brakes at no charge. This was rather a hollow victory, however. Despite a Congressional

135

investigation of the case, no crime was ever prosecuted, and those who had participated in the fraud were all promoted in the company.

Another case was reported to the present author at first hand. An employee of a large car manufacturer was responsible for recommending acceptance of bids for provision of car components. There were several bids on a particular component. The employee toured the plants of the bidders, and concluded that the low bidder had the best product to offer. He thereupon recommended that the low bid be accepted.

A short time later, the employee received a call from a vice-president of his corporation in Detroit (the employee was working in Wisconsin). There was a problem. The high bidder, whose quality control had been found to be inferior to that of the low bidder, was a subsidiary of the employee's corporation. The employee was directed to rewrite his recommendation to justify acceptance of the bid of the subsidiary. This struck the employee as (a) unethical, (b) fraudulent and (c) a violation of the United States antitrust law. He told the vice-president that the report would have to stand as already written. The vice-president ordered the employee to change the report or resign. The employee resigned. Subsequently, he heard that the contract had been given to the subsidiary.

An impression commonly left by those who have been involved in corporate management is (a) that amoral, appropriative activity in the service of corporate profit is commonplace, (b) that the corporate employee does not retard the activity by refusing involvement, but only gets demoted or fired, (c) that if the employee turns against the corporation and aids in prosecution for some of the activity, interruption or disruption of the activity is at best only temporary, and (d) that enough people involved in such activity get rewarded and escape negative sanction to provide sufficient positive reinforcement of the activity.

The impotence of any individual to retard such activity is particularly striking. The impotence extends even to presidents of large corporations. If a president makes his or her disapproval of such activity well known, one of two things can be expected to happen. Either subordinates, anxious to impress the president and other superiors with their profit-making ability, continue the activity and keep it concealed from the president (as the president of General Electric alleged had happened in the electric company conspiracy), or the president will be replaced by a board of directors, themselves responsible to shareholders, who want more effective leadership in the profit-making effort. It would be a rare president, especially of a large corporation, who could have risen to his or her position without prior cooperation in such activity anyway. For the corporate employee with qualms of conscience about such activity, the moral is apt to be that nothing is to be gained by open opposition and that the involvement of someone like himself or herself with at least pangs of conscience is the best of all possible worlds. The more typical attitude seems to be represented in a statement made to Vandivier by one of his superiors: '. . . I have no control over this thing. Why should my conscience bother me?' (Vandivier, 1972:19).

Hence, reliance on criminal law to locate and sanction individual employees for corporate wrongdoing has apparently proved generally ineffective in the United States. The wrongful activity has proven to be greater than any individual or few individuals within the corporation. That the problem is larger than accounted for by placing individual responsibility has suggested resort to the second approach – fining the corporation itself for corporate wrongdoing. A number of jurisdictions in the United States make corporations themselves liable for certain crimes. The corporations were convicted and fined under federal jurisdiction in the electric company conspiracy cases.

As a matter of fact, the fines in the electric company conspiracy cases illustrate one of the problems of this approach. It is hard to fine a large corporation enough to make the sanction serious. General Electric was fined $437,500 (see Geis, 1968:105), but this was less than two-thousandths of 1 per cent (0.0002) of the company's annual income (see Geis, 1968:106).

Even if the fine is large enough to constitute a serious sanction, the effect of the sanction on the conduct of corporate employees can be expected to be minimal. On the contrary, the pressure to generate additional profits to compensate for the loss can be expected to be the salient force on employees. The good and enterprising employee may deem it wise to take unusual pains to keep illicit activity concealed, but not to avoid illicit activity. The fine, after all, is no blemish on any particular employee's respectability. No finger of guilt has pointed at any individual, and the corporate ethos described above lends itself to a glib and easy denial of responsibility by any single employee. Since the need to contribute to increased profit margins is apt to outweigh the need to assuage guilt for the typical employee of a fined corporation, fining the corporation cannot be expected to affect corporate behaviour appreciably.

A third problem of the approach of trying to attach criminal liability to corporations themselves is that the laws providing criminal liability typically carry over a form of the common-law requirement of establishing individual responsibility for the crime. The Oregon Criminal Code (1971: sec. 161.170) provides an illustration:

(1) A corporation is guilty of an offense if:

(a) The conduct constituting the offense is engaged by an agent of the corporation while acting within the scope of his employment and in behalf of the corporation and the offense is a misdemeanor or a violation, or the offense is one defined by a statute that clearly indicates a legislative intent to impose criminal liability on a corporation; or

(b) The conduct constituting the offense consists of an omission to discharge a specific duty of affirmative performance imposed on corporations by law; or

(c) The conduct constituting the offense is engaged in, authorized, solicited, requested, commanded or knowingly tolerated by the board of directors or by a high managerial agent acting within the scope of his employment and in behalf of the corporation.

Note that paragraphs (a) and (c) require individual responsibility of an individual to be established before the corporation can be found criminally liable. Paragraph (b), the only one not to establish this condition, deals only with omissions, not with affirmative acts. Thus, when it comes to affirmative injury caused by corporate activity, the administrative problems remain of establishing which individuals are responsible for the injury, to prove the guilt of the corporation.

Hence, a proposal for legislation of negative incentives against specified corporate activity must overcome three difficulties of existing formal written criminal law on corporate wrongdoing. First, a way must be found to locate a responsibility for the activity that transcends individual employees. Second, the law must nevertheless establish that each employee whose actions might have contributed to the activity is held responsible before the law despite rationalisations to the contrary. Third, establishing responsibility for corporate wrongdoing must avoid any condition of identifying particular individuals who have chosen to engage in proscribed activity.


## Proposed Legislation

D.   *It is proposed that the criminal law provide that if corporate activity or activity carried out under real or apparent corporate authority is found to be a cause but for which legally specified social injury would not have occurred, every employee of the corporation and every person owning any interest in corporate assets (except an employee or person providing evidence leading to successful prosecution of the corporation for the activity) will be fined a fixed percentage of his, her or its gross income (including fringe benefits) received from the corporation. A corporation is a 'person' for purposes of this provision. The optimal percentage of the fine remains to be determined, as do specifications of social injury.*

The first clause of the proposal is designed to overcome the difficulty of pinpointing individual responsibility for injurious activity. If too many pollutants issue from a factory owned by the corporation, for example, there will be no need to decide which employee or employees are responsible for the 'activity' producing the injury. Defining the activity in terms of its injurious consequences will probably be held to be constitutionally permissible in the United States (see Oklahoma Criminal Court of Appeals, 1925).

Lest the defence be raised that injurious activity was not that of the corporation, it need only be shown that it was reasonable for an outside observer to presume that the activity was corporate, by virtue of the 'apparent authority' provision. Responsibility is thus thrust upon the corporation for taking care that legally specified injury that might reasonably be attributed to any actions of people on its behalf does not occur. The burden is placed on the corporation to control against the injury rather than upon administrators of the law to pinpoint exactly how the corporation as a whole or someone in particular in the corporation knowingly brought about the injury. Attaching corporate criminal liability even to expressly forbidden, apparently uncontrollable acts of its agents has been held to be a legislative prerogative (see United States Court of Appeals, Ninth Circuit, 1972, relying for imposition of corporate liability on reasoning of the United States Supreme Court, 1958, imposing partnership liability under similar circumstances).

While it has been held legally permissible to hold a corporation or other employer criminally responsible for the acts of its agents, attempting to hold employees and shareholders personally liable to fine for the crimes of their corporation is unprecedented, except in cases in which those employees found individually liable have been shown specifically to have had *mens rea*. Application of this provision might well be held by the courts to be an impermissible derogation of the due process rights of employees and shareholders under the Fifth or Fourteenth Amendment to the United States Constitution. Corporate criminal liability for acts of agents has been founded on the premise that the corporation can reasonably be held to control the conduct of its employees in the course of business. For the courts to accept the proposal made here, the premise must be accepted that employees and shareholders *collectively* can reasonably be held to control the activity of the corporation.

It is fair to say that if employees and shareholders *collectively* cannot reasonably be held responsible for corporate activity, that activity cannot reasonably be expected to be controlled by anyone. If the corporation is to be controlled, it can only be by employees' exerting that control. If any employee is to exert a control on corporate activity, it can only occur provided the other employees also have a vested interest in supporting rather than undermining that effort. An employee desiring to prevent corporate activity that might result in criminal liability must be able to show other employees who are prepared to participate in the activity that they too have a personal stake in refraining from participation. If those employees in high management positions are to meet their mandate to shareholders to give the shareholders income, it must be clear that the shareholders will suffer clear losses from activity that might otherwise seem expedient to increasing their investment income. If an employee would decline participation in questionable activity, mere moral misgivings can apparently be expected to be an inadequate justification in the eyes of other colleagues or superiors. The employee needs to be able to say, 'Look, if I do this, no matter how well concealed my role in the activity is, not only do you stand to suffer a personal financial loss, but so do I. For the pay I receive, the company may reasonably demand a loyalty higher than my own moral scruples. However, that argument depends on my being paid, not on my paying out of my own pocket to support the business. No one has the right to demand that I contribute to the income of the business out of charity, but that is just what I would be doing if I end up having to pay the state compensation for this activity out of my own pocket.'

In a sense, the argument for holding employees and shareholders indiscriminately responsible for corporate crime is circular. It is reasonable to hold them responsible because the law that holds them responsible gives them a basis for exercising responsibility.

The proposed exception to liability makes the imposition of collective liability still more reasonable. The exception encourages employees and shareholders to make it their business to be as well informed as possible concerning the possibility that criminal corporate activity is being carried out. It offers a further incentive not to tolerate such activity, and provides a means for an employee or shareholder to get outside assistance to bring the activity to a halt. For many activities, it gives control capacity even to those who are not in managerial positions. The assembly line worker who is told to change machine settings to those below legal standards, or any worker who sees such settings, has the information necessary to bring illicit activity to a halt and to be legally rewarded for so doing. The secretary who overhears calls or takes memoranda of illicit transactions has similar power. Even without going to state authorities and risking loss of employment, the worker who discovers illicit activity is in a strong position to demand that the activity cease 'or else'.

In sum, the negative incentive embodied in the proposal is designed not only to make everyone with a direct interest in corporate activity his or her own keeper, but his or her own brother or sister's keeper as well. Rather than inducing employees and shareholders to abdicate responsibility for control over illicit corporate activity, the proposed legislation might induce attempts to take that responsibility. Rather than reinforcing the sense that corporate activity is either a matter of purely individual responsibility or a matter of collective responsibility in a rather meaningless abstract sense, the application of the proposed legislation might reinforce a sense of collective concern for avoiding illicit activity at a rather concrete and personal level. Strength might be lent to motivation for interpersonal cooperation in making corporate activity responsible to popular concerns.

141

*Conclusion*

The proposal suggests that legislation of a negative incentive in the form of collective punishment might well deter specified kinds of injurious activity more effectively than can be expected of American criminal law in its present form. That would represent more effective social control of a kind through law, to be sure. But it also appears that legislation of negative incentives cannot overcome another problem: the one initially raised in chapter 2 as an inherent bias in the legal definition of social injury. Legislation like that proposed in this chapter would still reinforce appropriative, competitive behaviour — channel it maybe, but not discourage it. There is no reason to believe that social mobility would be curtailed by such legislation. Though greater effort at compliance with the law might be expended among the population, the elimination of elements of intent and of *mens rea* would more than compensate by facilitating criminal prosecution, and crime rates could be expected to continue to grow in the competitive popular milieu.

This result would be fascinating, for it would suggest that the law could be a general deterrent to perceivedly criminal behaviour while still amplifying rather than preventing officially recognised crime. There is a resurgence of popularity of classical utilitarian deterrence theory among American criminologists (see, for example, Zimring and Hawkins, 1973), and support for the idea that deterrence and crime could grow together would doubtless be a source of scholarly distress. Scholarly distress is a devilishly fun circumstance to contemplate, but perhaps better avoided.

If the growth of crime is to be curtailed, it appears that legislation of positive incentives is to be favoured over that of negative incentives. In so far as they succeeded in crime control, the positive incentives would tend to alter a broad range of cultural beliefs and patterns of behaviour in the United States. Without further interference, the new beliefs and behaviour patterns would be apt to assume the inertia of cultural tradition with the passage of time. It seems that persistent reduction of American crime rates would be no small, no isolated matter. If such a policy is to be pursued effectively, it has a number of implications which have not yet received much popular consideration in the United States. Though it is not an object of this study to commend crime control in an American setting, a new and complex approach to thinking about the problem is commended nevertheless.

# REFERENCES

Cameron, Mary Owen. 1964. *The Booster and the Snitch: Department Store Shoplifting*. New York: Free Press.

Geis, Gilbert. 1968. 'The heavy electrical equipment antitrust cases of 1961', in Gilbert Geis (ed.), *White-Collar Criminal: The Offender in Business and the Professions*, pp. 103–118. New York: Atherton Press.

Oklahoma Criminal Court of Appeals. 1925. *Miles v. State*. 30 Okla. Crim. 302.

Oregon Criminal Code. 1971. 'Criminal liability of corporations'. ORS, sec. 161.170.

Smith, Richard Austin. 1961. 'The incredible electrical conspiracy'. *Fortune*, 63 (April):132–180, and (May):161–224.

United States Court of Appeals, Ninth Circuit. 1972. *United States v. Hilton Hotels Corp. et al.* 467 F.2d 1000.

United States Supreme Court. 1958. *United States v. A & P Trucking Co.* 358 U.S. 121.

Vandivier, Kermit. 1972. 'Why should my conscience bother me?', in Robert L. Heilbroner, Morton Mintz, Colman McCarthy, Sanford J. Ungar, Kermit Vandivier, Saul Friedman and James Boyd, *In the Name of Profit*, pp. 3–31. Garden City, New York: Doubleday and Company, Inc.

Zimring, Franklin E., and Gordon Hawkins. 1973. *Deterrence: The Legal Threat in Crime Control*. Chicago: University of Chicago Press.

PART IV

# A Concluding Note

# 10. CONCERNING AGGRESSION

One lesson learned early in the study of patterns of rational response to criminal law is that the law cannot restrain administrators or a general populace from the pursuit of personal interest. The law can merely serve to channel the pursuit of those interests. No matter how many or how specific, the terms of the criminal law provide ample areas of discretion for administrators to optimise their personal interests, and for members of the general populace to negotiate with the administrators for their own gain also.

It is in the interest of American administrators in a competitive society to take jurisdiction over cases and apply the law as often as they can. The only indication that has been developed as to how much the United States needs administrators is simply an extrapolation of how much administrative services have cost in the past. A smart police administrator, for instance, knows that the more the offences officially reported in his or her jurisdiction the larger will be the departmental budget. The patrolman expects quite reasonably that the more arrests he or she makes, the greater will be his or her personal advancement. Hence, administrators in their work tend to pursue personal interest by selling more of their services to the general populace. Their success in this effort implies an ever-increasing rate of officially recognised crime in the social system.

How is popular demand to be created for these services? Once again, personal interest must be appealed to. People learn that they can turn to administrators for support of the priority of their claims to future access to resources on the one hand, and for allaying the personal cost of resolution of interpersonal conflict on the other. In this way, American administrators and the general populace sustain one another.

The proposals in this book are not designed to curtail the pursuit of personal interest. They are designed to rechannel that pursuit, so that

147

instead of being led to profit at others' expense, people are led to profit by virtue of the profit of all other immediately interested parties (known respectively in game theory as a zero-sum and a mixed-sum game). To rechannel the popular pursuit of personal interest, in such a way as to reduce crime, the law must provide an alternative incentive structure to that currently provided by formal written criminal law. The law needs to provide support and encouragement for people making strange new attempts to manage their interpersonal disputes among themselves. When the law provides a monetary benefit to some, the benefit must be based on the gain, not the loss, of other parties in interest. When the law penalises someone, it must be a burden that other parties in interest, including administrators, share. To effect reduction of crime rates, the law must be so structured that people who rely on it for personal gain look to do so *with* others to the practical exclusion of doing so *against* others.

It may be said of the proposals in this book that they represent a call for nothing less than a change in the nature of mankind. Inferences about 'natural laws' of human behaviour have gained some currency, and prominent among these notions are that people naturally tend to be aggressive toward one another. More than three centuries ago, Hobbes (1909) wrote that people tend 'naturally' to war against one another unless externally restrained. Recently, Lorenz (1966) concluded that people tend 'instinctively' to aggress against one another, although admittedly there is debate on this point (see Sullivan, 1974). The popular notion in the field of sociology of deviance that people typically label others as deviant and punish them in order to define in-group boundaries can be traced to Mead (1918). There is a sense pervading this genre of literature of the inevitability of people purposely trying to hurt other people. Given this sense, one is led to conclude that appropriation and interpersonal conflict, competition and punishment must also inevitably pervade any complex social system. One is led to reason that the law cannot be used as an instrument to change this 'fact of life' − that there is no good in people for law to help bring out, only bad for law to help restrain. The law can perhaps 'civilise' interpersonal violence − for instance, reducing homicide in favour of imprisonment − but the violence must ever continue. Anyone who believes that interpersonal competition and conflict can be rechannelled through law to emerge as interpersonal cooperation may be said to have a 'naïve faith in the goodness of

148

human nature'.

Though vague, the terms of this argument provide a powerful rationale for tolerance of a societal quota of crime and criminals (see Erikson, 1966) and continued growth of application of the kind of criminal law Americans now have. Unless the argument is plausibly assailable, political support for this kind of reliance on law cannot reasonably be expected to wane, while the kind of proposal made in this book can be expected generally to be dismissed as 'utopian' (an unfortunate appellation perhaps; even the originator of this term thought that diminution of selfish acquisitiveness required a measure of legal suppression — More, 1965:63—86).

Hope for the viability of proposals to reduce crime through positive enforcement of interpersonal cooperation rests not so much on eliminating aggression in people as on changing the *objects* of aggression from other people to social conditions. To illustrate, let interpersonal aggression be given a concrete referent. In economic terms, the assumption of inherent human aggression would take the form of assuming people to be innately or irrevocably acquisitive, such that any person is expected inevitably to direct his or her activity toward maximising access to use of economic resources. Assume further, as it has been for purposes of this study, that each person will adopt the optimal strategy for such maximisation, given the information available. What issues would then be involved in choosing whether to move from interpersonal competition to interpersonal cooperation as a dominant pattern of behaviour?

Two general strategies suggest themselves from which any person might choose the optimal path to personal gain. One is to minimise the access of others to resources in favour of one's own hegemony. The other is to maximise the access of others to resources without attempting to establish personal hegemony. Formal written law in the Weberian sense is a guarantee that administrators of the law will under specified circumstances act to protect one's hegemony, or right to exclusive use of resources (see Weber, 1967:5). Such a legally protected right is commonly known as a 'property right'. If, then, one chooses the first strategy, one will want formal written law so structured that it can be relied upon to protect one's own property rights. In the language of chapter 2, a choice of the first strategy implies a choice of participation in a system of appropriation which the law is structured to help to maintain. Selection of the second strategy, on the other hand, implies a

149

choice of avoidance of participation in a system of appropriation and a restructuring of the law to help provide alternatives to such participation. Choice of the first strategy implies use of law to help stabilise the salience of class distinctions (as discussed in chapter 7) while choice of the second strategy implies use of law to help break down class distinctions. The first strategy implies interpersonal competition, while the second implies interpersonal cooperation. Choice of the first strategy leads to support for the official finding and labelling of criminals, while choice of the second strategy implies resistance to institutions supporting this practice.

Choice of strategies rests essentially on whether a person prefers to risk wasting resource development capacity or misplacing trust in interpersonal support. An opponent of the competitive strategy would argue that attempts to establish hegemony tie up tangible resources (such as labour and material) in production and maintenance of property rights, which are useless in themselves. A property right cannot feed someone who is hungry; it cannot shelter someone who is cold; it cannot transport someone to food or shelter; it cannot provide someone with information; it cannot stimulate the senses in an aesthetically pleasing way like music or a book or a picture or a sculpture. At best, a property right can be a means to enjoyment of these resources. However, if resources were not devoted to production and maintenance of property rights, the resources could be used to produce more useful goods and services. Hence, to someone favouring the cooperative strategy, production and maintenance of property rights is a waste of production capacity.

In addition, production and maintenance of property rights is a waste of consumption capacity. It is inefficient for someone to be hoarding a resource when someone else might use it for immediate consumption. In short, both for production and consumption purposes, efficiency increases as the cost of people's access to tangible resources is reduced, and production and maintenance of property rights serves to increase that cost. As the cost of access to tangible resources is reduced, consumption and production capacity increase for everyone collectively and, therefore, in the long run, tend to increase for everyone individually.

Advocates of the competitive strategy would counter that unless distribution of resources is governed by property rights, production and consumption capacity will be wasted on fights over access to immediate use of resources and on enforcing organised production of other resources. Property rights are held to be necessary to permit each person to consume resources unmolested by others who want to consume. Efficient production at our level of technology requires that each person's production be specialised — that each person produce primarily for others rather than for personal consumption. Unless the producer is given property in exchange for the product, there will be no incentive for such altruism. The property system also provides the organisational foundation of a division of labour, without which labour cannot be coordinated in a technologically advanced social system. Hence, production and maintenance of property rights is conceded to be an expense, but the expense is held by proponents of the competitive strategy to be a necessary one to ensure optimal availability to each person of tangible resources. People cannot be trusted to coordinate economic activity for their mutual benefit without relying on the production and maintenance of property rights. In other words, because the predominant attitude of people toward one another in a social system such as that found in the United States is one of *distrust* of personal predisposition to share consumption of resources and to maximise altruistic productivity, the competitive strategy is the preferred strategy there. Causally speaking, interpersonal distrust and reliance on the competitive strategy are symbiotically linked.

This suggests an alternative to the economic aggressiveness that now tends to take the form of a battle for personal hegemony over future access to resources in the United States. In the battle for hegemony, people are the primary target of each other's aggressions. But if successful employment of the cooperative strategy were to become an American goal, the condition of interpersonal distrust would become the primary target of popular aggression. Interpersonal trust is requisite to experience of consumption and production of resources without resort to formal legal declarations of what is yours and what is mine — that people can get along together in their daily routines without devoting resources to clarification of who has hegemony over future access to resources.

If American law can be made to provide external support for people to learn norms of interpersonal trust to displace legal guarantees of a social order in which property rights are formally arranged, the level of interpersonal trust among the populace might grow to the point of making the cooperative strategy seem practicable to many Americans.

151

Were that to become the case, it would not imply a change in people's aggressiveness, but in the objects of their aggression. It would become less necessary and more wasteful to devote current resources to ordering future resource allocation; the ordering could feasibly be more nearly *ad hoc* and more flexible. The proposals in this book are designed to promote the growth of experience in interpersonal trust, utilising the habit Americans seem already to have developed of reliance on legal guidance.

Thus, if the proposals in this book are realistically feasible, it is not necessarily because mankind can be made characteristically less aggressive than now may appear to be the case. There is a chance that the substance of law can help to bring about a significant reduction in official rates of crime and criminals in American society — a chance based on the assumption that any aggressiveness in mankind's nature can be channelled from expression in aggression of people *toward* one another to aggression of people *with* one another to get more from the environment for everyone. Given the frustration Americans have experienced in trying vainly to resolve their 'crime problem' by the application of criminal law as it has existed in their society, perhaps the potential gains of proceeding on this chance are worth at least the risk of one more failure to control the growth of crime.

REFERENCES

Erikson, Kai T. 1966. *Wayward Puritans: A Study in the Sociology of Deviance.* New York: John Wiley and Sons, Inc.
Hobbes, Thomas. 1909. *Leviathan.* London: Oxford University Press (reprint of 1651 edn).
Lorenz, Konrad. 1966. *On Aggression.* New York: Harcourt, Brace and World.
Mead, George Herbert. 1918. 'The psychology of punitive justice'. *American Journal of Sociology*, 23 (March):577–602.
More, Sir Thomas (Peter K. Marshall, trans.). 1965. *Utopia.* New York: Washington Square Press.
Sullivan, Walter. 1974. 'German researcher in behavior suggests that violence is culturally based'. *New York Times* (26 March):18.
Weber, Max (Edward Shils and Max Rheinstein, trans.; Max Rheinstein, ed.). 1967. *Max Weber on Law in Economy and Society.* New York: Simon and Schuster, Inc.

# INDEX OF AUTHORS
(italicised numbers refer to reference pages)

154

Van der Sprenkel, S.   38, *43*, 80, *90*
Vandivier, K.   135–6, 137, *143*
Veblen, T.   42, *43*

Wallerstein, J. S.   106, *115*
Weber, M.   83, *90*, 99, 103, *105*, 106, *115*, 149, *152*
Weir, A. W.   *69*
Wenk, E. A.   107, *115*

Westley, W. A.   57, *70*
Wilson, J. Q.   59, *71*
Wolfgang, M. E.   58, *71*, 109, *115*
Wyle, C. J.   106, *115*

Yang, C. K.   80, 86, *90*
Yee, A. H.   95, *105*

Zeisel, H.   53, *55*
Zimring, F. E.   142, *143*


# INDEX OF SUBJECTS

155